The Drawing Room Symphony

A history of the piano duet transcription

Ian Shepherd

Published by Kingswood Publishing
Norwich, England

Copyright © Ian Shepherd 2008

British Library Cataloguing in Publication Data. A catalogue record
for this book is available from the British Library.

ISBN 978-0-9560730-0-6

Kingswood Publishing

Contents

Introduction

The huge growth of the piano duet repertoire that began at the turn of the nineteenth century and was sustained for well over a hundred and fifty years, is one of the most interesting, yet largely unexplored, phenomena in the history of Western keyboard music. Transcriptions of chamber and symphonic works made up a sizable chunk of this repertoire and despite being staple fare in musical households of the Victorian period and beyond, are today almost entirely forgotten.

Often regarded as second-rate salon music, of little historical or musical interest, piano transcriptions – especially those for duet (two performers playing upon one instrument) – have consequently received little academic discussion. There are, of course, some notable exceptions – the transcriptions and concert paraphrases of Liszt (1811-1886), of which there are several hundred and the piano arrangements of symphonies by Brahms (1833-1897) are frequently cited. Yet, a vast array of composers engaged in arranging and adapting chamber music, symphonies, ballet suites and similar works for piano duet. This book concentrates mainly upon composers who adapted and arranged their own work but also discusses the work of a number of specialist arrangers.

The practice of arranging music for piano duet positively flourished in the nineteenth and early twentieth centuries. There was a ready market for duet publications as piano ownership became commonplace. As Louis Kentner states:

'The all-purpose nature of the instrument opened up the way for its spectacular invasion into drawing rooms all over the world, an invasion which lasted for over a century. The piano was an integral part of every self-respecting household.' [1]

4

A piano transcription allowed access to music that was, for the most part, inaccessible. Before the invention of the gramophone and radio, those who were unable to hear symphony or chamber music concerts used four-hand arrangements to familiarise themselves with the music of the great composers. In many ways, these published transcriptions were the equivalent of our recorded music collections today.

One can view arrangements for the piano in two ways. Stripped of orchestral colour, they can only offer a 'monochrome' listening experience, the myriad detailing of the original score diluted to the extreme. On the other hand, a piano reduction allows the listener to focus upon the essential elements of the composition, so that its component parts become more immediate. Paul Serotsky asserts that:

'Stripping off the luxuriant upholstery of the orchestration exposes the harmonic nerves, the melodic guts and the rhythmic skeleton of the music. By peeling off some of the wrappings we might see more of what's inside the package.'[2]

Given over a half-century of neglect of this repertoire and the lack of research in this area, it is not surprising to find that much of the music is now 'lost' in the sense that it is now generally unavailable or extremely difficult to find. In an age when such arrangements were deemed as being of little worth, many were simply thrown away. As well as public institutions such as libraries and university music departments, publishers too removed a vast array of duet transcriptions from their shelves, particularly in the 1950s and 60s. For example, Novello, the London music publisher, following several mergers and changes of premises, discarded the vast majority of their piano transcriptions in the knowledge that at least one copy could be found in the British Library. Sadly, today, Novello have no existing records of transcriptions originally published by them.

As publishers have merged, gone out of business, catalogues of works bought and sold, much of the history surrounding many of these transcriptions has been severely eroded. The famous Kalmus catalogue, which contains a sizeable number of duet arrangements of symphonic works, is now owned by the Alfred Publishing Corporation, after changing hands several times since these works were originally published. Although the original engraving plates survive, the vast majority of the supporting documentation relating to these duets is now lost and therefore the various arrangers are mostly unknown or cannot be identified with due certainty.

As a result, it is not surprising to find that there is often a mixture of confusion, uncertainty and inaccuracy in documentation relating to piano duet transcriptions. Most commonly, original composers are credited with making transcriptions which were actually made by others and works written for two pianos are referred to as piano duets. The modern trend to perform duets on two pianos – as adopted by some leading 'duettists' – has generated some further confusion.

To compound matters, most of the 'in-house' arrangers employed by the major publishing firms of the nineteenth century are unfamiliar – most not even receiving the briefest mention in the 'New Grove Dictionary'. One might surmise that the fact that they have been largely over-looked is a clear indication of the perceived value of their work. Even one of the most prominent figures in nineteenth century music publishing, Robert Keller (1828-1891), editorial assistant to Brahms and producer of numerous transcriptions for the great publishing house of Simrock, has no entry.

Whilst this book does not aim to be a totally comprehensive survey of the four-hand piano transcription genre, it is the first publication to discuss the subject in some detail, rather than just list known transcriptions. Whilst these lists are invaluable, often indicating the effectiveness and suitability for performance of transcriptions, they offer only a partial guide to the subject. Hopefully this book will give the reader a greater insight into an area that has been severely neglected so far.

The Transcription

Surprisingly, the term 'transcription' has no absolute meaning and one can find several different definitions, often with subtle but significant changes, in a range of music dictionaries and encyclopaedias. However, most academics concur that transcriptions are essentially a sub-category of the wider term 'arrangement'.

Whereas a transcription always involves a change of medium, an arrangement does not. However, both may be for smaller, larger or even similar forces. Whilst a transcription does not have to be an exact copy of the original – there is the opportunity to make adaptations which make it more suited to the new medium – it should remain, in essence, faithful to the original. The terms 'transcription', 'arrangement' and 'reduction' are, for the purposes of this book, largely interchangeable.

It could be argued that the first transcriptions originate well before the development of musical notation, thousands of years ago. As simple vocal lines were adapted for the earliest primitive instruments, a process was developing, allowing for the adaptation and re-arrangement of music.

Since the earliest notated music appeared, there have been numerous examples of music written in one form being adapted for other mediums, whether it be through a process of transcription, adaptation, parody or pastiche. As new instruments were developed, as well as writing new works specifically for that instrument, older works were re-drafted and, in many cases, further embellished to suit.

Even the earliest recorded composers 'borrowed' from each other and adapted music that was not their own. The common practice of intabulation where works originally written for several instruments or singers were transcribed for a single instrument (usually the lute or organ) can be traced as far back as the fourteenth century. There exist, for example, several organ arrangements of vocal motets in a manuscript from Robertsbridge Abbey in Surrey (c.1350) and other similar documented works in the fifteenth and sixteenth centuries. It is therefore not surprising that the true authorship of some early music cannot be verified.

In the Baroque period, transcription was a common practice, followed by most of the leading composers. J. S. Bach (1685-1750), for example, made keyboard transcriptions of many orchestral and concertante works by such composers as Vivaldi (1678-1741), Albinoni (1671-1751), Marcello (1686-1739) and Telemann (1681-1767).

Whatever the musical era, the transcription satisfied a number of purposes, including that of making the music more accessible. Piers Hellawell comments that:

'The professional and amateur musician of the Romantic era relied on chamber media, in particular the piano duet, as the means of reproducing orchestral and operatic works when live performances were sparse indeed. The making of piano reductions was a practical solution to a terrible problem – the inaccessibility of large works.'[3]

Even those able to attend orchestral performances were not always entirely happy with the experience. The typical nineteenth century concert hall was cold, damp, smelly (the combined effects of tobacco smoke, poor drains and gas lighting), cramped and full of distractions. The ability to play orchestral works at home through the medium of the piano transcription therefore offered the typical middle class family a decidedly more comfortable experience.

The piano became the ideal instrument for transcription. Berlioz (1803-1869) commented that 'the piano can be seen in two ways: as an orchestral instrument, or as a complete little orchestra in itself.'

9

Anton Rubinstein (1829-1894) added that 'a piano is not just one instrument – it is a hundred.' Dieter Hildebrandt comments that:

'The piano emerged as the as the tried and tested *universal instrument*. It could trace the outline of a string quartet just as surely as it could probe the structure of a symphony.'[4]

Musical purists might object to transcriptions on the grounds that an original work of art is sacrosanct and ought never to be tampered with. This rather implies that the musical 'integrity' of the original work is somehow compromised by the production of a transcription. However, all such arrangements have one thing in common, which is true whether they set out to simply reflect the original as faithfully as possible, to make what might be properly called a 'transcription' or, at the other end of the spectrum, set out to completely 're-think' the original piece. This common factor is that if the music is 'arranged' in any way, it becomes, to a lesser or greater extent, a different piece of music, which should be judged on its own merits. Roger Scruton makes the point that a piece of music will naturally undergo a process of change as it becomes more widely known:

'The process of musical dissemination creates versions, variants and transcriptions as a by-product. We make an intuitive distinction between the transcription which is the same work of music as the original, and the transcription which is another work, derived from, but not identical with, its parent. The ruling intention of the transcriber is to preserve the pattern of pitched sounds as the composer intended it, but without the instrumental colour.'[5]

Transcriptions were often used to evaluate a new work, a famous example being that of Schumann (1810-1856), who wrote an extended analytical review of the *Symphonie Fantastique* Op. 14 by Berlioz from a study of the piano transcription produced by Liszt, rather than the full orchestral version. This is, in part, testament to Liszt's genius as an arranger for the piano.

10

Even if a full score was available to a critic, a piano duet arrangement was often the only means of actually hearing the work. It was therefore seen as being perfectly legitimate to review a new work based solely upon the transcription. If a reviewer had been lucky enough to attend an orchestral performance, the piano duet transcription would allow him to further evaluate the work. Robert Keller commented that a four-hand transcription allowed those who had attended a concert:

'to investigate the fine lines of the drawing while the magnificent colour of the whole is still fresh in their minds and to delight in the abundance of attractive and ingenious details that are simply impossible to grasp in their entirety during the first exciting hearing of the original.'[6]

Indeed, piano duet transcriptions were seen as an ideal medium for testing out compositions before their full – orchestral – performance. The first English performance of Brahms' *Ein Deutsches Requiem* Op. 45 was the piano duet version given on July 10 1871, at the home of Lady Thompson (formerly Kate Loder 1825-1904), a prominent pianist of the day and teacher at the Royal Academy of Music. She was accompanied by the English composer Cipriani Potter (1792-1871) and a large number of 'ladies and gentlemen'. This preceded the first full performance, given by the Royal Academy. Brahms made much use of this procedure.

Edward George Dannreuther (1844-1905) was another wealthy and cultured individual who organised a series of semi-private chamber concerts held at his home at Orme Square, London, which introduced works by Brahms, Tchaikovsky (1840-1893), Rheinberger (1839-1901), Stanford (1852-1924), Parry (1848-1918) and Richard Strauss (1864-1949) to English audiences for the first time. Dannreuther played Tchaikovsky's First Piano Concerto Op. 23 in a two piano arrangement (sanctioned by the composer) before its first 'official' hearing at Crystal Palace with Dannreuther as soloist in

March 1876. Before this full, orchestral performance, Dannreuther wrote to Tchaikovsky suggesting amendments to the piano part (which Rubinstein famously described as being 'unplayable'). Tchaikovsky responded positively and revisions were duly made for the second edition of the score.

 **Edward George Dannreuther, founder of the 'Orme Square' concerts.**

A few years later, in 1887, Bruckner (1824-1896) heard his Fifth Symphony in a version for four hands in Vienna. He had to wait another seven years before its first orchestral performance took place and, sadly, was too ill to attend. As will be seen later, the piano transcription played a fundamental role in the eventual acceptance of Bruckner as a composer of great distinction.

As recently as the mid-twentieth century, some composers relied on piano transcriptions to familiarise others with a work in progress. Vaughan Williams (1872-1958) was one such composer who had a reputation for spending a great deal of time revising his work. His one-time amanuensis, Michael Mullinar (1895-1973), made a two piano version of the Fifth Symphony from a very sketchy score so that the composer could hear it played (recounted in a letter written by the English composer, Thomas B. Pitfield (1903-1999) to Michael Kennedy in 1962). For the Sixth Symphony which was actually dedicated to Mullinar, Mullinar made both a solo piano and two piano reduction.

Byron Adams describes one of Vaughan Williams 'testing out' sessions:

'On 10 June 1947, Vaughan Williams arranged for a series of four private auditions of the [sixth] symphony at the Royal College. These performances were given for an invited audience of about forty colleagues and conductors in order to seek their advice concerning technical and formal details of the new work. The pianist on this occasion was Michael Mullinar. Mary Mullinar remembered that her husband copied out the score he used for the Royal College performances directly from Vaughan Williams's holograph short score. Roy Douglas, who was Vaughan Williams's musical assistant from 1944 until the composer's death in 1958, was present at these performances. Douglas recalled that Mullinar performed from a complete solo piano version of the score.'[7]

Only a fragment of this score remains and was given to the library of the Royal College of Music and catalogued there in the late 1980s.

Transcriptions were often viewed as having educational merit, often promoted as such by the various publishers, purchased for study as well as performance. Many concert-goers would enhance their experience by investing in a piano reduction either before or after a concert. Of the piano duet, Thomas Christensen says:

'It was truly the primary vehicle of musical literacy not only in the nineteenth century, but well into the twentieth. Over and over musicians – amateur and professional alike – testified to the value of playing piano transcriptions in promoting their musical literacy.'[8]

Indeed, Wagner (1813-1883) is said to have stated that, as a student, transcribing the Ninth Symphony Op. 125 by Beethoven (1770-1827) for piano was one the best composition lessons he had ever had. Wagner sent his manuscript to the publisher Schott in 1830 – they were to publish it 160 years later as part of the *Complete*

Wagner Edition (1990 onwards). Interestingly, unlike Liszt, whose celebrated arrangement incorporated the solo voice and choral parts into the piano texture, Wagner only reduced the orchestra, leaving the vocal lines intact.

Certainly, the practice of both preparing and performing transcriptions was a fairly routine academic exercise in most of the European conservatories of music. The piano had become the ideal vehicle for advancing musical education. As late as the 1930's, Gordon Jacob (1895-1984) advocated the use of duet transcriptions for orchestral scoring practise, mentioning works such as the *New World* Symphony Op. 95 by Dvořák (1841-1904), Tchaikovsky's *Pathétique* Symphony Op. 74 and the *Enigma Variations* Op. 36 by Elgar (1857-1934). He also advised students to compare the orchestral versions of works such as Brahms's *St. Anthony Chorale* Variations Op. 56a and Henri Busser's orchestration of the *Petite Suite* by Debussy (1862-1918) with that of the original piano versions.[9]

However, even a 'routine academic exercise' is not without difficulty. As Michael Steinberg comments:

'Good transcriptions are not easy to make. Like any sort of translator, the musical transcriber can be suspended in excessive literalism by reverence or sheer lack of imagination; on the other hand, carelessness, irrepressible creative impulses, irreverence, or an inclination always to know better can lead to risky departures from the original.'[10]

In discussing transcriptions, it is useful to consider the processes involved in producing such arrangements.

A transcription will, most likely, be produced using the full orchestral score as reference. However it is quite feasible that quite the opposite may sometimes be the case. The composer or arranger must make the decision as to how literal the transcription should be. This has always been a source of some contention between composers, arrangers and publishers.

Unlike a transcription for solo piano, in a duet transcription there is scope for including the full range of pitch utilised in the original orchestral work as four hands can cover lower, middle and higher registers simultaneously. Thus a duet arrangement can successfully present strident brass chords in the middle register, a deep sustained bass line and support an upper-register woodwind melody. A two piano transcription (as opposed to one piano) gives the arranger even more scope. Towards the end of the nineteenth century the two piano eight-hand transcription enjoyed some limited success. However, repertoire was very sparse and the difficulties of putting on a domestic performance – with the need for two pianos and four competent pianists – was extremely constraining.

The percussive nature of the piano and its inability to sustain notes for any great length of time also needed to be addressed. Long sustained notes or chords lasting for several bars, originally played by strings or woodwind, for example, are difficult to replicate on the piano. Thus the composer or arranger must decide on a method to 'suggest' the intention of the original. Notes or chords may be repeated or a tremolando effect employed. However, over-used, the latter can be tiresome to listen to.

Although one piano cannot hope to match the full dynamic range of an orchestra, judicious use of dynamics in the piano reduction can enhance the impact of the work. The careful use of the sustaining pedal, and where applicable, the sostenuto pedal also adds to the overall effect. There is an immediacy to the piano sound and, in music with a contrapuntal texture, the listener can focus entirely upon the interweaving and layering of the melodic lines, undistracted by the variation of timbre of the original.

Most orchestral music relies upon this variation of timbre and the creation of tone colour to achieve an impact. Given that a melodic line originally given to an oboe, or clarinet or French horn will sound exactly the same when played on the piano, there is little that the composer or arranger can do to suggest differing timbres.

The perceived value of the piano transcription in all its forms began to wane in the early years of the twentieth century. Discussing Liszt's arrangements of songs by Schubert (1797-1828), Alan Walker states:

'By the beginning of the twentieth century... Urtext was the thing. Scholarship pressed its case with evangelical zeal, and was extraordinarily successful in converting a whole generation of musicians to the idea that only the original 'soundscape' was worthy of attention. The crime of an arrangement now was that it *was* an arrangement. It had no interest in preserving original sound. Moreover, it often played fast and loose with the notes. Since it flouted the Urtext it had to be condemned as second-class music. Between the two World Wars, few pianists ventured onto the concert platform to play a Liszt arrangement. Out of temper with the times, a whole repertory of wonderful music was hushed up and forgotten.' [11]

Certainly, a more scholarly and rigorous approach to music publishing had an impact upon the popularity of the transcription, but there were other factors in play too. As a medium, radio was becoming increasing popular and the market for recorded music was growing at a tremendous rate. It was no longer necessary to play the music yourself in order to hear it. From around the 1930s, four-hand piano transcriptions fell from grace in spectacular fashion for a period of almost sixty years.

Writing in 1927, Percy Grainger (1882-1961) expressed his dismay at this demise:

'When Brahms wanted to hear a new symphony of his own composition he did not call together a whole orchestra there and then. He arranged it for two pianos and played it with Clara Schumann. Ravel and others willingly spend their time arranging works for two instruments. Grieg did so, too. If those men have been willing to make arrangements of their own compositions in this manner, and not only the compositions of others, why should the smaller flight, who really hardly know anything about anything at all, make such an uproar against arrangements and transcriptions? They merely doom themselves to the night of ignorance instead of joying in comparative knowledge. When we have become familiar with the great works of all times and countries through the medium of arrangements and transcriptions, we will find ourselves the more ready for the reception of those works in their original scoring. What we really have to think about is the interest of the works themselves, and not the quality of the sound.'[12]

However, from the mid-1980s onwards there has been a gradual 'rehabilitation' of the genre. Ivan Raykoff states that:

'The piano-arrangement repertoire has never completely disappeared from recital programs, even during the modernist and authenticist mid-century. But piano transcriptions and paraphrases have enjoyed a vigorous renaissance in recent decades, as witnessed by the increasing numbers of recordings and concert programs that feature these works. Evgeny Kissin included the Schumann-Liszt *Widmung* in his 1990 Carnegie Hall debut recital. Stephen Hough's 'Piano Albums' of 1988, 1993 (both Virgin Classics), and 1999 (Hyperion) feature numerous transcriptions, including some of Hough's own.'[13]

Not only have transcriptions from the past been seen in a more favourable light but new transcriptions are now being published. One such example is the *Suite for Strings* by Frank Bridge (1879-1941). Completed in 1910, the work was published ten years later and a piano duet version was prepared, though this was never actually published and the manuscript considered lost. To commemorate the fifty years since the death of the composer, the Frank Bridge Trust commissioned Hwee San Tan to prepare a duet version of the work, which received its first performance in October 1991.

The four-hand transcriptions made by Jonathan Fisher of several of the player-piano studies of Conlon Nancarrow (1912-1997) are another notable example. Supposedly 'unplayable' by humans in their original form, Fisher has managed to capture Nancarrow's numerous layers of detail in his transcriptions, but, even with two players, some elements have been difficult to accurately reproduce, such as the enormous span of some chords and the exact duration of notes (though the initial placing of the notes can be performed accurately). Even more recent are the four-hand transcriptions made by the pianists Dennis Russell Davies and Maki Namekawa of music by Steve Reich (*Piano Phase*) and Philip Glass (six excerpts from the 1996 dance opera *Les Enfants Terribles*, originally written for three pianos and four voices).

With renewed interest being shown by both performers and audiences, there has also been a growth of previously unpublished transcriptions being made available. One of the most recent and important examples is the piano transcription made by Bartók (1881-1945) of his *Concerto for Orchestra*, written in 1943. Bartók was offered the sum of $500 to transcribe the work for piano, for use in ballet rehearsals, as the New York Ballet Theatre wished to perform the work. It took Bartók just three weeks to complete the task, transcribing each orchestral page in just two hours. Although written out for single piano, Bartók recommended that the score be played by two pianists, especially in the more complex passages:

'Small-head notes are added which mostly cannot be played by one player, in order to give a more complete picture of the work. For making the gram. record, it would be advisable to have it played by two pianists, the second playing the small-head notes. This, of course,

18

is not absolutely necessary, for the parts with big-head notes give also a sufficient idea of the music. Except in the last movement from [482] to [555]. This portion is impossible to transcribe adequately for one piano.'[14]

The transcription was found in 1985 by the composer's son, Peter, who asked the pianist György Sándor (1912-2005), who had studied with Bartók and remained a life-long friend, to edit the manuscript. It was published by Boosey & Hawkes in 2001.

It is most interesting to compare Bartók's original orchestral score with his own transcription and Sándor's subsequent revision. As already mentioned, Bartók sped through the task of transcribing the work and therefore we see a somewhat rough-hewn arrangement – practical but not especially idiomatic. However, one might argue that this approach leads to Bartók capturing the essential essence of the work – fresh and vital. Indeed, Bartók only ever made one copy and what we see on his manuscript are essentially his first thoughts. By contrast Sándor's revision is more considered and he is more creative in reducing the full orchestral forces to just two staves.

It is most certainly true that there are a number of transcriptions of similarly important works awaiting discovery and eventual publication and Roger Scruton reminds us of the fact that transcriptions still have a value today, despite the vast legacy of recorded performances of the entire musical spectrum:

'By playing Beethoven symphonies in an arrangement for piano duet, you come to understand them as tonal structures, in a way that is increasingly difficult for people whose only experience of these works is through polished performances on polished discs.'[15]

Indeed – if we are to really know the music, to inhabit its inner core, is there any better way to do this than to actually perform it?

Sándor at the piano with Bartók. Sándor recorded all of Bartók's piano works, winning the prestigious 'Grand Prix du Disque' in 1965.

The Development of the Piano Duet

The rise in popularity of the piano duet is inextricably linked with both the technical development of the piano and its increased use in the domestic situation.

Most scholars agree that the earliest known pieces for two performers at one keyboard date from the early seventeenth or possibly late sixteenth century. These are examples of the English 'fancy': *A verse for two to play* by Nicholas Carlton (c1570-1630) and *A fancy for two to play* by Thomas Tomkins (1572-1656).

Carlton and Tomkins were close friends and neighbours in Worcestershire and it is probable that these pieces could have been composed for them to play together on the virginal – an instrument with a range of only five and a half octaves. At that time, the virginal was a relatively popular instrument, with Samuel Pepys referring to a large number being rescued in the Great Fire of London.

Very little keyboard duet music was written during this period. Both the harpsichord and clavichord were not particularly well suited to duet writing, being too small to accommodate two players easily and of limited compass. Social conventions also had a part to play in the relative scarcity of the duet – the close proximity of the players being rather too daring in the middle class establishments of the time. The act of touching hands, almost inevitable in duet playing, was particularly frowned upon with some publishers of duet music issuing 'rules of etiquette' in an attempt to avoid this faux pas. Clothing of the period was elaborate and often restrictive – the demise of the wig, corset and hooped skirts towards the end of the eighteenth century had a positive impact upon the popularity of the piano duet.

Several composers left the decision to perform a piece on one instrument or two to the performers themselves. Several of the Suites by François Couperin (1668-1733), though written for one keyboard, state that they are 'ideally suited for double-keyboard performance.' Moreover, Couperin often indicated in the Preface to his scores that any combination of instruments was acceptable. Bernardo Pasquini (1637-1710), a largely forgotten Italian composer, wrote a huge amount for keyboard. His Fourteen Sonatas (1704) contain several marked as being 'for one or two cembali'.

With its clear advantages over both the harpsichord and clavichord, the piano – being able to respond dynamically to changes of force with which the keys are struck, capable of sustaining a wider range of notes and having the strength of tone for it to successfully accompany other instruments or voices – quickly grew in popularity in the eighteenth century amongst the growing numbers of affluent middle class families as well as the gentry and aristocracy. Renowned piano manufacturer, John Broadwood (1732-1812) extended the range of the keyboard from five to six octaves in 1791 and, by 1803, added another half an octave. These keyboards become known as 'duet range' – much more suitable for two players. Seven octave keyboards became common from 1850 onwards and by 1870, the eighty-eight note piano we know today had become standard. This expansion of range was, in part, a direct result in the increasing popularity of the piano duet medium.

Haydn (1732-1809) did much to popularise the piano duet. His F major Divertimento *Il Maestro e lo Scolare* (*The Master and the Pupil*), has been dated to 1766-1768. Specifically designed for teaching purposes, as its title suggests, the opening theme, very similar to the Handel keyboard piece that later became known as *The Harmonious Blacksmith*, is played by the master and echoed by the pupil, phrase by phrase. This procedure is broadly followed in the eight subsequent variations. The versions of the theme, as they proceed, introduce slightly greater demands for digital dexterity and allow the teacher to occasionally elaborate without being echoed by the pupil.

At around the same time, the English composer, Charles Burney (1726-1814), published a series of pieces entitled *Four Sonatas or Duets for Two Performers on One Piano Forte or Harpsichord.* The first edition was a great success, with a second edition being printed, the following year, 1778. In the preface to the first edition, Burney offered some useful advice for playing duets:

'As the following pieces are the first that have appeared in print it may be necessary to say something concerning their utility, and the manner of performing them.

That great and varied effects may be produced by Duets upon Two Keyed-Instruments, has been proven by several ingenious compositions, some of which have been published in Germany; but the inconvenience of having two Harpsichords, or two Piano-Fortes, in the same room, and the short time they remain exactly in tune together, have prevented frequent trials, and even the cultivation of this species of music, notwithstanding all the advantages which, in all other respects, it offers to musical students.

The playing Duets by two persons upon One instrument is, however, attended with nearly as many advantages, without the inconvenience of crowding a room, or of frequent or double tunings; and so extensive is the compass of keyed-instruments, that the most full and elaborate compositions must, if played by one person, leave many parts of the scale unemployed; which, perhaps, first suggested the idea of applying Pedals to the Organ. And though, at first, the near approach of the hands of the different performers may seem aukward [sic] and embarrassing, a little use and contrivance with respect to the manner of placing them, and the choice of fingers, will remove that difficulty.'[16]

Burney goes on to discuss other problems related to duet playing such as understanding balance, treatment of harmonic and melodic textures (in order to bring out the 'Principal Melody'), accuracy regarding ensemble and so on. His comments are just as valid today as they were when written, well over two hundred years ago.

Charles Burney — a pioneer of the early duet.

The first years of the nineteenth century were dominated by the Napoleonic Wars. During this period, a number of wealthy European families suffered severe financial hardship, resulting in them disbanding their 'house' orchestras and chamber groups. The pianoforte became the replacement orchestra, the piano duet the ideal medium for symphonic transcriptions. By the mid-nineteenth century, the piano was a fixture in most Victorian middle class households — an important catalyst in the developing domestic social revolution. Piers Hellawell comments that:

'Duet playing was the clearest manifestation of the spirit of domesticity without which any small ensemble music is ersatz. The humblest piano duet represented something much greater than its content — not just the presence of music in the home but the intimacy of collaboration, in an age when other intimacies, particularly between the young, were kept in check. It is not far-fetched to see in the unselfconscious domesticity of vocal and duet music around the piano a highly active forerunner of our passive participation in television today.'[17]

The domestic piano of choice was most usually the upright piano (grand pianos were marketed as being primarily for concert hall performances), the manufacturers of which numbered hundreds. By 1900, it is estimated that London alone had over one hundred and fifty piano factories and nearly five hundred music shops selling instruments.

Much of this success was linked to the various commercial connections that were forged by leading 'players' in the piano manufacturing industry. For example, Muzio Clementi (1752-1832) became a partner in both a music publishing business and a piano manufacturer as his career as a virtuoso began to wind down. Friedrich Kalkbrenner (1785-1814), celebrated virtuoso, teacher and composer who contributed a number of original piano duets to the repertoire, invested in the Pleyal piano factory, making a huge fortune as a result. This had been set up by the composer and publisher Ignaz Pleyel (1757-1831). A pupil of Haydn, he was a prolific composer of keyboard duets, some original and some being arrangements of his chamber music. Other virtuosos, such as Henri Herz (1803-1888), founded their own piano factories around Europe. Dieter Hildebandt comments that:

'Virtuoso experience was to be passed on not just to students but also to instrument-makers. Teachers were as much concerned with the mechanics of the piano as with techniques of positioning and fingering. This close connection between theory and practice, between piano-playing and piano-making, demonstrates more clearly than anything else that the pianoforte was the communal product of a great number of interested minds — a favourite field of experiment for amateur tinkers and professional virtuosos, for mechanics and musicians, for salesmen and teachers.' [18]

There is a persuasive argument to support the belief that the four-hand repertoire developed largely as a result of need and circumstance. J.S. Bach, for example, composed duets to allow his sons to play together in family musical gatherings – his sons, in turn would go on to compose sonatas and concertos for four hands themselves. The Sonatas written between 1778 and 1780 by J.C. Bach (1735-1782) are particularly notable examples. Mozart (1756-1791) composed duets as a result of him spending much of his childhood performing in concerts with his sister Nannerl. As children, Mozart and his sister had given what is claimed to be the first public duet recital, held at Hickford's Great Room, London in 1765. His four-hand Sonata in C (K.19d) was probably written for this occasion. The famous painting by de la Croce shows Wolfgang and his sister sitting at the piano, playing a duet. Mozart went on to play duets with Hummel (1778-1837), Marianne Martinez (1744-1812) and Ignaz von Beecke (1733-1803) with whom he performed one of his last public recitals in Frankfurt in 1790. Clementi enjoyed performing in public with his pupil, John Field (1782-1837) and composed seven Duet Sonatas specifically for these concerts. Mendelssohn (1809-1847), like Mozart, wrote duets for himself and his sister to play. Brahms had close friendships with several other pianists, often playing duets with them.

Nannerl, Wolfgang and Leopold Mozart c.1790.

However, most performers were amateurs, usually playing for their own amusement. There were, no doubt, some outstanding players amongst them, but the standards of the average player should not be over-estimated. For many, solo transcriptions of symphonies, opera excerpts, string quartets and the like, were far too difficult. The piano duet format was generally less taxing for individual players. In any case, solo transcriptions, by their very nature, had to forgo many of the complexities of the original. The duet transcription provided an almost perfect medium.

If one were to compare the numbers of original works written for piano duet in the late eighteenth, nineteenth and early twentieth centuries, with those arranged (in all guises) for the medium, one would find that the latter vastly outnumber the former. Looking at the output of the great composers from this period, it is evident that the piano duet was not a particularly favoured genre. Most composers famed for their output for piano wrote a mere handful of works for four hands. Commenting on the Brahms' piano arrangements, Ates Orga states that:

'While the repertory may overflow in arrangements, it is surprisingly wanting in original music. Single volumes of Mozart (significant) and Beethoven (less so), three volumes of Schubert (seminally important), some Schumann (variable), the four books of Dvořák *Slavonic Dances* (indispensable) grace most pianos — but that is about all. Given such paucity, Brahms' contribution, dating largely from between the early (1852-66) and late (1892-93) solo piano works, is the more to be prized.'[19]

Only Schubert wrote a substantial amount of original works for the medium — justly considered masterpieces of the duet repertoire. According to his brother, Ferdinand, Schubert's first composition was a piano duet written in 1810.

One might have expected Schubert to transcribe a number of his symphonic works for piano duet but this was not the case. The orchestral *Overture in the Italian Style* D.590 was transcribed for piano duet by the composer (D597) but little else. Robert Schumann thought that the Sonata in C Major for Piano Four Hands (the *Grand Duo* D812 composed in 1824) was a piano arrangement of a symphony, though there is no documentary evidence to support this. Brahms shared this view, even persuading the violinist Joseph Joachim (1831-1907) to orchestrate it in 1855, in order to let people hear 'how it is was meant to sound.' However, Schubert did leave some substantial piano sketches of projected symphonic works, including several attempts at a D Major symphony (D615, 1818, D708A, 1820-21, D936A, 1828).[20]

The growth and popularity of the piano duet is almost entirely down to the social importance of the piano in the domestic situation of the time. Duets were to be played at home, primarily for entertainment, rather than being destined for the concert hall. Bernard Holland states that:

'As the nineteenth century unfolded, a relatively new musical invention was being developed into a cultural utensil increasingly reliable, affordable and numerous. Musical performance began to leave the palace and enter the middle class parlour. The piano was the Romantic era's television set. Sheet music, often in the form of duets, was its software. If a family in Grenoble, Gutersloh or Philadelphia wanted to hear the newest Mendelssohn symphony and no concert hall was nearby, there was always a reduction for the keyboard for family members to bang out for themselves at home.'[21]

Indeed, John Rockwell, music critic of The New York Times has called duets the 'ultimate parlour game.' The less numerous body of work composed for four hands on two pianos was more likely to receive a concert performance, it being rather unlikely that one household would contain more than one piano.

Given the thirst for repertoire and the paucity of original material available, the duet arrangement thus began its meteoric rise – a publishing phenomenon unequalled in the history of Western classical music. By the mid-nineteenth century, some of the largest music publishers were turning out arrangements on an almost industrial scale.

The advent of sound recording combined with the eventual demise of the piano transcription had a profound effect upon the piano duet genre as a whole. Lois Svard Burge comments that by the early twentieth century, this form of music making seemed 'destined for oblivion'.[22] Discussing the role of the piano duet, Piers Hellawell states that:

'The nineteenth century duet's everyday 'recording' function kept it in the picture, giving rise to original masterpieces such as Schubert's *Fantasia* or Mendelssohn's *Variations* Op. 81a along the way. With the lapse of its functional role, the duet fell into disuse – what composer has turned to it since Ravel and Fauré?[23]

He goes on to accept that there are a few notable exceptions to this such as the Sonata for Piano Duet by Poulenc (1899-1963) and several sets of original duets by Stravinsky (1882-1971).

Hellawell may be rather glib in this matter, yet the essence of his argument rings true. Whilst many composers have dabbled with the piano duet format, few have written anything more than a handful of works. Today, it could be argued that the genre survives largely on the basis of what has been written in the past rather than because it has a contemporary relevance. A study of music publisher catalogues reveals the current situation quite clearly. Whilst one will certainly find new four-hand repertoire being published, it is most likely to consist of yet more arrangements of popular classics – more often than not of an elementary nature, geared towards the teaching market.

However, looking beyond the surface, one can find a significant number of works written especially for (or commissioned by) specific duettists. Indeed it could be argued that this 'composed for' duet repertoire is the very lifeblood of the genre in the late twentieth and twenty-first centuries. The husband and wife piano duet team of Ethel Bartlett (1896-1978) and Rae Robertson (1893-1956) – one of the first ever established professional duettists, gaining international recognition in the 1920s – had a number of pieces composed for them by such composers as Britten (1913-1976) who wrote the *Scottish Ballad* Op. 26 for them and Bax (1883-1953) who wrote a series of original pieces in the 1920s such as *The Poisoned Fountain* and transcribed several of his works for the duo, including his *Festival Overture*. Bartlett and Robinson went on to edit the 'Two Piano Series' of transcriptions and arrangements for Oxford University Press.

A few years later, the duettists Phyllis Sellick (1911-2007) and Cyril Smith (1909-1974) rose to prominence, and, following a stroke in 1956, which paralysed Smith's left arm, a new repertoire of three-hands music was created for them by such composers as Lennox Berkeley (1903-1989) and Malcom Arnold (1903-2006) who composed his Two Piano Concerto (Three Hands) Op. 104 for them. Many four-hand works were subsequently 're-cast' for three. In 2007, Faber Music commissioned John Lenehan to 'transform' the Two Piano Concerto into a straightforward piano concerto (for one performer at the piano), in order to increase its popularity in concert performances.

More recently, duettists such as Katia and Marielle Labeque, David Nettle and Richard Markham, Isobel Beyer and Harvey Dagul and Anthony Goldstone and Caroline Clemmow have all had works especially commissioned for them and revived neglected duet repertoire.

The Bartlett — Robertson piano duo.

Perhaps, ironically, the past is actually the key to the future of the piano duet. As mentioned earlier, one can surmise that countless manuscripts of duet arrangements, yet unpublished, must exist in various public and private institutions. The sheer numbers of those that reached publication suggest that there were many that didn't. One can envisage that, in due course, these will be discovered and made available, thus supplementing the duet repertoire, already dominated by transcriptions of various sorts. Thus the piano duet, inextricably linked with the transcription, has an interesting future as well as an illustrious past.

Composers and their Publishers

One particularly important area to consider, and one which is very often overlooked or underplayed, is the economic framework of the music industry, the relationship between composer and publisher and the actual mechanics of publishing in the nineteenth and early twentieth centuries.

Such considerations relate to virtually all music of this period, but are absolutely fundamental to the understanding of the growth of the piano duet and other piano transcriptions.

It was in the eighteenth century that many of the leading publishing houses were established. Given the musical importance of the Germanic composers at this time, it is not surprising that most of these firms were German in origin. Breitkopf of Leipzig was founded in 1754 (Härtel joined the firm in 1795), Schott Music of Mainz was founded in 1770, Simrock of Bonn (later Berlin) was established in 1790. In Vienna, Artaria began music publishing from 1778. Between them, they published most of the leading composers of the day.

The process of printing music was, in the eighteenth century, elaborate, expensive and prone to inaccuracy. Movable type had already revolutionised the printing of the written word, but printing music required far greater complexity. The difficulties of integrating notes and other markings with the stave often resulted in an expensive two or three stage printing process. The stave would be printed first, then another print would add notes and a final print added the other markings. This necessitated the perfect alignment of the paper, which could not always be guaranteed. Breitkopf's initial success was largely founded upon developing a better typesetting process ('mosaic' type) which resulted in high quality printed scores being produced.

Such a development allowed publishers to issue far greater numbers of works that could be printed at a much lower cost. With the invention of lithography (in Germany in the late 1790s) and photo lithography (as early as 1839), the printing process was further refined, costs further reduced and so began the mass commercialisation of printed music.

Today, we have, perhaps, an over-romanticised view of classical music. We see composers as being largely successful, greatly respected and somehow free from the domestic drudgery and demands of everyday life. Although the vast majority came from what we could term as 'middle class' backgrounds, wealth was certainly not excessive and composers needed to earn a living – either by patronage, commission, teaching, conducting and so on. The publishing industry became another vital source of income from the mid-eighteenth century onwards, which, in a number of cases, had a strong influence upon the output of the individual composer.

Up until the beginning of the eighteenth century, copyright did not effectively exist. It was not until 1709 (the Statute of Ann) that measures were brought in to establish the principles of copyright and the ownership of intellectual property in England. A work was protected for a period of 21 years (later extended to 28). Other European countries followed afterwards, each with its own set of laws. However, it was not until as late as 1886 (the Bern Convention) that an international accord was reached.

Before this time, composers had little protection from their work being published by others and therefore gaining nothing for their creative endeavours. The absence of effective copyright laws made it possible for a publisher to make arrangements, in any form, of any work he could acquire – legitimately or not. It was not uncommon for an unauthorised arrangement to be put on sale before the composer had chance to make his own.

The *Seven Last Words* Op. 51 by Haydn (1732-1809) was originally scored for full orchestra, and was premièred in that version in 1787. Whilst the orchestral parts were being printed, Haydn's publisher persuaded him to transcribe the work for string quartet, which Haydn readily did. However, a suggestion that the piece could be re-worked for piano drew a less than enthusiastic response from Haydn. Nevertheless, his publisher went ahead and produced a piano version. Rather than oppose this, Haydn decided to cooperate on the project and read the proof copies, making corrections as necessary.

In 1801, Haydn wrote to August Eberhard Müller (1767-1817), the Leipzig Kapellmeister who was making a piano reduction of *The Seasons* stating that a particular passage had to be corrected in order to leave out a bit of word-painting. He wrote:

'This whole passage, with its imitation of a frog, did not flow easily from my pen; I was forced to write down this French swill. With the whole orchestra this miserable idea disappears rather soon, but it cannot remain in the piano score.'[24]

Disputes between composers and publishers were common. For example, Beethoven had a very public disagreement with the publisher Henning concerning an unauthorised piano duet version of *The Ruins of Athens* Op.113 issued in 1825. Beethoven was particularly annoyed because he had just sold the overture to another publisher (Schott) who subsequently issued solo piano and piano duet versions made by Carl Czerny (1791-1857). Henning refused the request to withdraw his publication and Beethoven retaliated by having a notice printed in a leading musical journal stating that Henning's version was not only illegal but of poor quality.

In 1889, Alexander Ziloti (1863-1945), a Russian pianist and composer and former pupil of Liszt, prepared a two-hand piano transcription of Tchaikovsky's *The Sleeping Beauty* Op. 66. He then arranged for the young Rachmaninov (1873-1943), his pupil at the

Moscow Conservatory, to prepare a four-hand version for the publisher Pyotr Ivanovich Jurgenson (1836-1904), for 100 roubles, to which Tchaikovsky agreed. Unfortunately, due to a series of delays, Tchaikovsky did not see the arrangement until the second proof stage. When these reached Tchaikovsky, he wrote to Ziloti:

'I have corrected the proofs of *The Sleeping Beauty* prologue and this task gave me considerable pain. You may say that a first proofreading can be done superficially, while the vital corrections can be made in the second proof, but it is the transcription itself that I do not like. We made a great mistake in entrusting this work to a boy, no matter how talented. This transcription has two horrible deficiencies:

1) Lack of courage, skill and initiative, too slavish a subordination to the composer's authority, depriving the work of force and brilliance.
2) It is too apparent that the four-hand transcription was made from the two hand transcription rather than from the orchestra score. Many details necessarily omitted from the [two-hand] piano score, though quite convenient and possible for the four-hand transcription, are missing here too. These proofs have so upset me that I haven't been able to sleep − I feel a sickness approaching...'[25]

Tchaikovsky scribbled his notes and alterations all over the score and sent it back to Ziloti, who, in turn, made the necessary corrections. This apparently pacified Tchaikovsky and good relations were restored between all three. Later, Rachmaninov commented:

'Tchaikovsky abuses me dreadfully for the transcription, quite reasonably and justly. Of all transcriptions mine is undoubtedly the worst'.[26]

Ziloti and Tchaikovsky.

Given the fact that printing music was still a relatively costly and time-consuming business, publishers were keen to ensure that any mistakes were corrected before engravings were made and editions printed. This necessitated a working dialogue between composer and publisher — one that was often fraught with tension.

One of the closest dialogues documented between composer and publisher is that between Brahms and Fritz Simrock (1837-1901). Brahms was able to use his position as undeniably one of the greatest of composers of his day to assert his influence over his publisher. Thus Simrock, though impatient, had to work at a pace dictated by Brahms, who was meticulous in the preparation of his work before publication. Brahms involved himself in every aspect of publishing, from the initial copying stages to the final print run. Such was his stature, he could successfully demand that editions be withdrawn due to small errors being spotted later — and a corrected edition being printed to replace it.

Otto Singer (1863-1931), a highly respected arranger for the Peters firm, came to Vienna in May 1904 to talk with Mahler (1860-1911) about the piano transcription of his Fifth Symphony. In the following two months, Mahler revised and corrected the arrangement. Henry-Louis de la Grange refers to a letter that Singer sent to Peters:

'It is a complete disaster. From day to day he changed his mind about the necessity of certain alterations, and ended up approving what initially he was about to reject, without taking any account of the mature reflection I had already given to each bar. In the last two movements, he at first decided every note was in place. Why then in the end did he change his view so radically? Once before I have had to withdraw my name from a transcription because I did not wish it to be misused to cover up for the clumsy bowdlerizations a young composer has foisted on to my work. Is it really necessary for me to do that again?'[27]

The publisher attempted to console Singer by reminding him that it was far better that corrections were made now, rather than after the work had been printed, that the composer's corrections were principally in the last two movements and that it was matter of just 'bringing out the trumpet part'. The first edition of the four-hand transcription comprised of six hundred copies. Mahler's earlier symphonies were initially printed in even smaller numbers – as low as one hundred and fifty copies. Many publishers preferred to reprint on a periodic basis rather than produce large numbers of copies which might not sell.

These relatively small print runs contrast greatly with the tens of thousands of copies made of the music of Verdi (1813-1901). For example, Ricordi published a whole host of reductions for piano and voice, solo piano, string quartet, various combinations for flute, violin, clarinet and piano as well as the piano duet from *Rigoletto*. From his other various operas, there were reductions and transcriptions of individual arias, cavatinas, choruses and overtures which could all be bought separately. The substantial revenues obtained allowed Ricordi to offer Verdi unprecedented sums for the publication rights to his operas. Additionally, Ricordi took on the business affairs of Verdi and a number of other composers, booking opera houses for performances, renting costumes and so on.

Not all composers were so well rewarded. Like Verdi's, Wagner's later operas were also published in various reductions. However, Wagner often had to agree to this purely as a result of financial necessity. These arrangements usually appeared before any first performance and the publication of the full scores. To some extent it can be argued that some composers were exploited by their publishers, not by any great malice, but by the sheer commercialism of the business. However, it should also be acknowledged that such publications did no particular harm and ultimately generated a wider interest in the music.

Having already had several years of success with the publisher Simrock, Dvořák nevertheless was no free agent. As a businessman, Simrock was most keen to publish songs and individual piano pieces which could be prepared and sold relatively easily. He was less willing to readily agree to publish full symphonic works. Indeed he refused to publish the full score of Dvořák's Seventh Symphony Op. 70 until a piano duet version was made. Writing to Dvořák, he said:

'If only I did sufficient business with your symphonies to be repaid for my enormous expense. I am thousands down on them. What use is it if I make money on one or six works and lose it again on four others? I cannot carry on my business like that! If the performances are successful, the composer thinks his work will sell. You were successful over the D Minor Symphony, but not a single copy, not even a piano duet version, was sold. So, unless you give me small and easy piano pieces, it will not be possible to publish big works.'[28]

Simrock did publish the Seventh Symphony but relations between composer and publisher soured even further with the Eighth Symphony Op. 88 and Simrock's derisory offer of 1000 Marks for the work (Brahms had been paid 40,000 Marks for his Fourth Symphony Op. 98). Eventually, Dvořák decided to break his contract with Simrock and sold the work to the London firm, Novello. Good relations were restored with Simrock by the time the Ninth Symphony Op. 95 was due for publication.

A book of letters exchanged by Frederick Delius (1862-1934) and Philip Heseltine (1894-1930) - later known as Peter Warlock, contains this correspondence, concerning the publisher Leuckart:

Letter from Philip Heseltine to Frederick Delius 6 January 1914:
'I am sending the piano arrangement of the *Song of the High Hills* to you by this post. If you have time to play it through, and mark in pencil what you would like altered, and then return it to me, I will make a fair copy of the work afterwards. I have transcribed chorus and orchestra together, attempting to get a *general impression* of the work on the piano. Of course the whole work is difficult and in many places unplayable, but I have thought it better to put as much as possible of the score into the arrangement, even at the expense of it's playableness, for I think one gets a better impression that way.

Of course, I should be very pleased indeed to have my arrangements accepted by Leuckhart, even if he paid nothing, since it would be a great help to me afterwards to have a specimen of my arranging in print, especially an arrangement of one of your works. It is really good of you to say will let me do your work, but I do hope you are really satisfied with my arrangements of them.'

Letter from Frederick Delius to Philip Heseltine 18 January 1914:
'Your arrangement of the S*ong of the h. h.* is wonderfully good in parts — you seem tho' to have hesitated between putting everything in & eliminating. I do not know much about piano arrangements but they must be playable & give a good idea of the work. Leuckart wrote to me that he would be willing to publish your two arrangements but could pay nothing for them!! These editors are awful people — I wrote back that you would let him have them for 75 Marks — so I am awaiting his answer.' [29]

Percy Grainger recalls that he fell in love with the music of Delius on the strength of hearing some of Heseltine's piano arrangements. Heseltine was a tireless editor of early music and made nearly six hundred modern transcriptions of ancient manuscripts. His most famous piece, the *Capriol Suite* for strings was originally written for piano duet in 1926. Grainger himself went on to produce several four-hand arrangements of Delius as well as many other four, six and eight hand versions of an eclectic mix of music.

One publisher who could not be accused of penny-pinching was the Russian Mitrofan Petrovich Belyayev (1836-1904), the son of a wealthy timber merchant and patron of the arts. The 'Belyayev Fridays' (also known as 'Les Vendredis') were a noticeable feature of the St. Petersburg music scene in the late nineteenth century. Composers such as Tchaikovsky, Rimsky-Korsakov (1844-1908), Glazunov (1865-1936), Liadov (1855-1914) and Scriabin (1872-1915) would meet at Belyayev's house to play chamber music – string quartets, trios, piano duets and so on. As well as playing established music, they also wrote pieces especially for these gatherings, including a number of collaborative compositions. Belyayev, keen to promote Russian music, also established the 'Russian Symphonic Concerts' series.

Belyayev was unhappy with the state of music publishing in Russia, where music was issued in poor quality editions, on poor quality paper and issues of copyright were unresolved. In 1884 he set up his own publishing house, which was heavily subsidised by his own personal wealth, in order to promote Russian music. This was based not in Russia, but in Leipzig, Germany, where the latest printing technology was available and copyright law was in force. He could afford to pay his composers generous sums and produce high quality editions, often featuring artwork by leading contemporary artists. As a matter of policy, all music was issued in three formats: full score, separate orchestral parts and, significantly, an accompanying four-hand arrangement. Publishing the latter as a matter of course allowed the music to receive a much wider circulation. Additionally, the duet transcriptions were issued with both English and Russian (Cyrillic script) titles and directions.

Belyayev's influence on late nineteenth century Russian music was immense.

This altruistic approach to publishing was very much the exception and as the twentieth century progressed, publishers became increasingly unwilling to invest in producing piano transcriptions of orchestral works. As the recording industry strengthened and catalogues of orchestral recordings increased, the mass market for piano reductions began to fall. The piano – once a focal point in the drawing room, was superseded initially by the gramophone and then the wireless (with music broadcasting starting in Europe and America from the early 1920's onwards). In America, sales of radios ($60 million in 1922) increased to over $843 million by 1929. In the same period, piano sales fell drastically, forcing the vast down-sizing of the industry. A similar situation occurred in Europe with a great deal of piano manufacturing companies going out of business, especially in the economic recession of the 1920's.

As has been already mentioned, publishers allowed a huge swathe of music to go out of print and, eventually, removed many existing publications entirely from their shelves. Often, original engraved plates were destroyed. However, like any other business during this period, the music publishing industry needed to adjust and respond to change. As demand for duet transcriptions faltered, publishers were no longer willing to pour money into a seemingly dying genre, focussing instead on producing more scholarly editions of original works, rather than transcriptions. This, in turn, lead to a growing perception that the transcription was a rather out-dated musical vehicle, no longer fashionable in the concert halls and, worse of all, of dubious taste.

In the last few years, with a growing interest in transcriptions, publishers are beginning to respond accordingly and, perhaps even more significantly, other means of making music available to a wider audience have emerged. This is discussed more fully in the final chapter.

Before 1800

As the piano grew in popularity in the late eighteenth century, the rise of the piano transcription began. The piano duet had now firmly established itself as a popular medium and it is therefore not surprising that many of these transcriptions were for four hands at one piano.

Arrangements of operas and symphonies were particularly popular. One of the first ever publications issued by Simrock, the German publishing firm that was to become one of the most important publishing houses in the nineteenth century, was a piano duet transcription of themes from *Das rote Käppchen* – an opera by Dittersdorf (1739-1799). Dittersdorf's more famous contemporary, Haydn, was a particularly popular composer with arrangers. Many individual movements from his symphonies were arranged for piano duet – the slow movements being especially favoured, perhaps reflecting the rather genteel nature of performance and domestic sensibilities at the time. The English publisher, Birchall, issued all of Haydn's *London* symphonies in duet format between c1798-1800. They sold extremely well, being reprinted several times. Mozart's music also proved popular, his clear, precise orchestral lines translating well to the piano duet medium.

The musicologist, Alexander Weinmann (1901-1987) made a study of Viennese music publishing in the late eighteenth century. He compared the number of piano solos published with the number of piano duets. He discovered that there were almost as many pieces for four hands as there were for two published during this period. His personal archive – one of the world's major collections of eighteenth and early nineteenth music publishing - is now held at Duke University, North

Carolina. Much of the duet material comprised of arrangements of symphonic material.

Significantly, these arrangements – and there were literally thousands of them published by the end of the eighteenth century – were not usually prepared by the original composers. This period saw the emergence of the professional 'arranger', tasked with the reduction of a vast array of orchestral music. Whilst it would be wrong to suggest that these transcriptions were rushed out without any real artistic consideration, it would be fair to say that these early transcriptions lacked the sophistication of those made in the following century. A relatively small number of arrangers were to develop the transcription very much in to an art form in itself.

The Nineteenth Century

Beethoven and Schubert

Any discussion of the nineteenth century should start with Beethoven, equally straddling the eighteenth and nineteenth centuries and being instrumental in forging the Romantic style. Beethoven, as we know, was an outstanding pianist, preferring to compose mainly sonatas, variations and concertos for solo piano, which he himself could perform. Surprisingly, the Sonata in D Op. 6, Marches Op. 45, Variations WoO 67 and WoO 74 and *Grosse Fuge* Op. 134 are the only duet works he composed. Apart from the latter, they are light in style and provide an interesting contrast with his more serious works.

Composing in an era where transcription was becoming increasingly common, Beethoven expressed strong views on the practice. In a letter to the publisher Breitkopf and Härtel in 1802, concerning arrangements of piano music, he wrote:

'The unnatural mania for transplanting piano stuff to string instruments, instruments so completely opposite in all ways, might well cease. I firmly maintain that only Mozart, also Haydn, was capable of translating himself from the piano to other instruments, and without wanting to set myself up as the equal of those great men, I would maintain the same thing about my piano sonatas. It is not just a matter of totally leaving out and changing whole passages. One also has to add, and there is the stumbling block: to overcome it you either have to be the master yourself or at least be his equal in cleverness and invention – I have transformed only one of my sonatas into a string quartet, for which I had been urgently asked, and I know for certain that no one else is going to come along and do it equally well.'[30]

The sonata referred to was the Sonata in E Op. 14 No. 1 and was not actually published until 1910.

Of particular interest is Beethoven's *Grosse Fuge*, a rare example of a piano transcription Beethoven made of one of his own works (the other notable example being the piano transcription of the Violin Concerto, known as Op.61a, which has a remarkable cadenza featuring the timpani as well as solo piano), which attracted international attention in 2005. The eighty page autograph manuscript, Beethoven's version for piano duet, thought lost for over one hundred years, was found in the library of the Palmer Theological Seminary in Pennsylvania, America and sold at Sotheby's, London, for £1,128,000. The buyer, Bruce Kovner has since presented this, together with his priceless collection of other manuscripts to the Juilliard School in New York.

Beethoven's manuscript of the *Grosse Fuge* on display prior to the auction. Schoenberg regarded the work as a 'premonition of atonality'.

The manuscript reveals a composer who revised constantly. There are smudge marks where Beethoven rubbed out the ink before it could dry, scratches where he erased notes with a needle and remnants of red sealing wax – used to paste in long corrections. The intensity of the composer can be seen graphically – the higher and more intense the music, the larger the notes. It also appears that Beethoven played through the music as it was written – page 23 contains, for example, Beethoven's own fingering solutions.

Originally, the *Grosse Fuge* was the final (sixth) movement of the String Quartet Op. 130 in B flat. However, reaction to this movement in particular was adverse. After the première, March 21 1826, given by the Schuppanzigh Quartet, one reviewer stated that the music was 'incomprehensible, like Chinese' and full of 'Babylonian confusion', suggesting that Beethoven's deafness was at fault. The Quartet members expressed their belief that the fugue was simply too demanding. Bowing to public pressure, Beethoven composed a new finale, agreeing to have the *Grosse Fuge* published separately (as Op. 133). Anton Halm (1789-1872) was commissioned to produce a piano duet transcription, which he duly sent to Beethoven in April 1826. Beethoven was so disappointed with the results that he decided to make his own arrangement — one of his final creative tasks before his death in 1827 — which was numbered Op. 134.

It is interesting to note the many differences between Op. 133 and Op. 134. Indeed, the very fact that Beethoven gave this arrangement a different opus number is significant, suggesting that this was not simply a straightforward transcription.

There are a great many changes of dynamic marking, many original *sforzando*s removed for the piano duet version, replaced by simple *forte* markings. The texture is thickened in many sections with the doubling in octaves of parts, particularly the cello. Beethoven even makes changes to the notes, seen most obviously in bars 28, 38, and 44, and moves parts up or down an octave several times. He changes many of the articulation markings and original rhythmic patterns are also altered. In its piano guise, the work sounds much more compact. The louder passages benefit from the stronger bass of the piano and the immediacy of the piano attack serves to make many of the rhythmically taxing passages more precise.

The piece is notoriously difficult to play — so much so that Beethoven's own transcription went quickly out of print. Harold Bauer made a two piano version in 1927, aiming to make the piece more accessible in this format but this transcription proved to be equally unpopular.

A number of Beethoven's works appeared in print as duet arrangements in his lifetime. Carl Czerny, pupil of Beethoven and teacher to many of the leading Romantic composers, arranged many of his works. For example, Beethoven entrusted Czerny with the task of producing the piano reduction of his opera *Fidelio*. The arrangements produced by August Eberhard Müller are particularly noteworthy due to the fact that Beethoven had a particular admiration for his work as both a composer, conductor and arranger. His duet transcription of Beethoven's *Eroica* Symphony Op.55 was published by Peters, Leipzig in 1814. One critic commented:

'Since there are so few orchestras complete and accomplished enough to perform such a difficult work suitably, and since even when one has heard it so performed, it is still very interesting to repeat this music to oneself on a good fortepiano, we will be grateful to the publisher and to Music Director Müller for having provided such a complete keyboard reduction so well suited to the instrument as one could expect from the insights and talents of Mr. M. on the basis of other similar works. The list of distinguished compositions for four hands is not extensive, and accomplished keyboard players will find rewarding work here.'[31]

The Seventh Symphony appeared in print in 1816, alongside keyboard arrangements (solo piano, piano duet and for two pianos) by Anton Diabelli (1781-1858) and Beethoven's final symphony, the Ninth in D minor Op. 125, commissioned by the Philharmonic Society (London) and first performed in 1824, was later arranged for piano duet by the Secretary of the Society, William Watts. The 1844 publication, printed by Chappell of London, was entitled *Beethoven's Grand Choral Symphony Arranged for two performers on the piano forte with accompaniments (ad libitum) for flute, violin & violincello, by W. Watts.*

There is a significant body of opinion that Beethoven's symphonies retained their popularity largely as a result of the fact that they were available in so many households in various piano transcription modes. Close friend of Beethoven, Johann Nepomuk Hummel's piano transcriptions of the symphonies, made between 1826 and 1832 were especially popular. Wagner wrote:

'If [the *Eroica*] today is received with acclamation almost everywhere, the sufficient reason, to take the matter seriously, is that for some decades past this music has also been studied outside the concert-room, especially at the pianoforte, and thus has found all kinds of circuitous routes for the exercise of its irresistible force in its no less irresistible fashion.'[32]

Beethoven's 6 octave Broadwood grand piano (serial number 7362), presented to him by Thomas Broadwood (1786-1861) in 1818. Later owned by Franz Liszt, it now resides in the National Museum of Hungary.

By the time of Beethoven's death, there had been a huge proliferation in the quantities of piano transcriptions available. Thomas Christensen refers to Adolph Hofmeister's frequently published nineteenth century catalogues of music that listed thousands of duet arrangements. Hofmeister (1802-1870), was the epitome of the publisher/businessman, preferring to print piano transcriptions which would sell in large quantities rather than publish full orchestral scores which had no mass market. Christensen states:

'Included among these publications are the ubiquitous parlour genres one would expect: waltzes, gallops, marches, fantasies, variations on popular songs, lyrical pieces, potpourris of opera tunes and the like. But also present are a large number of transcriptions of more sober concert repertory. With approximately 150 entries, Beethoven is one of the standout composers (second only to Czerny), with all of his symphonies, overtures, string quartets, and other chamber music transcribed. (There are in fact three different arrangements of each symphony to choose from.) But ambitious pianists could also find transcriptions of pieces we might not ordinarily think of as idiomatic to four-hand performance, such as the five piano concertos, the masses, and the complete score of *Fidelio*. Even the thirty-two solo piano sonatas were available from the Litolff firm in a duet arrangement by Louis Köhler.'[33]

Köhler (1820-1886), was known as a pianist, conductor, teacher and composer. A pupil of Liszt, he is today remembered best for his large output of piano studies and methods.

This latter example illustrates clearly that a number of transcriptions were made on wholly commercial rather than artistic grounds. Cameron McGraw states:

'It is interesting to note the lengths to which some tasteless merchants have been willing to go in order to take full advantage of the lucrative four-hand market. Since all music was fair game and every composition, great or small, was potentially marketable in some format, over-eager publishers occasionally pushed their enterprise to ludicrous extremes.'[34]

Eager to maximise profits, some publishers issued newly revised transcriptions on a periodic basis — each one stating that it was somehow more 'musical' or 'authentic' than the last. Whilst it is the case that some arrangements improved upon others (the Czerny versus the duet transcriptions made by Hugo Ulrich (1827-1872) of

Beethoven's symphonies for example – the latter being generally considered the better), a great number were issued for purely commercial reasons.

As has already been mentioned, Schubert, surviving Beethoven by only one year, produced original duet compositions rather than transcriptions. Highly marketable, the publishers Probst and Artaria both demanded duet works from Schubert in order to satisfy public demand.

Following his death, there came a number of transcriptions made by others. Schubert's celebrated *Trout* Quintet D667 was published just after his demise by Joseph Czerny (1785-1831), Czech composer and publisher alongside his own piano duet version of the piece. The latter, long out of print was recently discovered by Anthony Goldstone in the Music Department of the Austrian National Library. The Library also uncovered a piano duet arrangement of the overture to *Rosamunde* D664 made by Josef Hüttenbrenner (1796-1882), one of Schubert's inner circle of friends. His brother, Anselm Hüttenbrenner, notorious for keeping Schubert's manuscript of the Eighth *Unfinished* Symphony D759 locked away in a cupboard, Schubert having sent him it in 1823, made a duet version of the work for his own pleasure before Johann Herbeck 'rescued' the work in 1865 and subsequently conducted its first performance in Vienna that same year. Carl Reinecke (1824-1910) produced the official duet transcription which was published by C. A. Spina alongside the full score in 1866. The *Trout* was again arranged for piano duet by the Dutch composer, Jan Brandts-Buys (1868-1939), who worked for the publishing house, Universal Edition in Vienna. He also arranged all of Schubert's symphonies for the medium, as well as transcribing the works of Beethoven, Mozart and others for duet.

Mendelssohn and Liszt

The generation of composers following Beethoven and Schubert were, perhaps, the most active in producing duet transcriptions of their own symphonic work, and it was Mendelssohn, one of the first-born of the great romantic composers of the nineteenth century, who produced a significant number of piano duet arrangements.

As already mentioned, Mendelssohn grew up playing piano duets with his sister, Fanny. Almost as precocious as Mozart, he studied piano with Marie Bigot (1786-1820), renowned teacher and friend of Beethoven, whilst living in Paris. Fanny, five years his senior, was considered by many to be as talented as her brother and an even better pianist. She composed a number of piano duets herself, though, like most of her output, these remained unpublished until relatively recently. Kassel published her *Three Pieces for Four-Hand Piano* in 1990. Fanny, in many ways, was Mendelssohn's musical mentor – the exceptionally strong bond between them revealed in the many letters and diary notes that she wrote. Given this, it is not surprising that Mendelssohn viewed the medium of the piano duet so favourably.

Fanny and Felix Mendelssohn.

The four-handed version of *A Midsummer Night's Dream* Op.61 was probably composed concurrently with the orchestral version – the Overture in 1826 and the other movements in 1843. The seventeen year old Mendelssohn took just one month to complete the Overture in November 1826. Following this, he gave a duet performance at a family concert, with his sister, Fanny.

However, it was not until 1832 that Mendelssohn decided to publish the Overture, sending both the orchestral parts and the duet transcription for printing. The London publisher, Cramer, Addison and Beale published the duet first, with the title *Overture to Shakespeare's Midsummer-nightsdream arranged as a Duet for two performers by Felix Mendelssohn Bartholdy*. Breitkopf and Härtel published the work the following year for the German market. An interesting eight-hand version was later made by Robert Keller, but, like most of the eight-hand repertoire, quickly went out of print.

The young Mendelssohn also had an additional duet partner in Ignaz Moscheles (1794-1870), Bohemian composer and piano virtuosi. As a teenager, Mendelssohn studied piano with Moscheles and they remained friends and duet partners until Mendelssohn's death. Referring to Mendelssohn in a letter, Moscheles wrote:

'What endless music we have made together! I made him play over and over again his own things, which I followed in the score. He would on these occasions imitate some wind instrument or take up a point in a chorus with his clear tenor voice. Whenever he has arranged one of his overtures as a pianoforte duet, we try it out over together, until we find it perfectly suitable for the piano.'[35]

Much has been written about the musical genesis of Mendelssohn's *Hebrides* Overture Op. 26. He made numerous small and large scale revisions before its final publication. Following a performance in London in May 1832, conducted by his friend and composer Thomas Attwood (1765-1838), Mendelssohn inscribed the date of 19 June 1832 on the autograph arrangement for piano duet and that of the full score. At this time the piece was known as *Overture to the Isles of Fingal*.

Mendelssohn arranged for the piano duet transcription to be published by the London firm of Mori and Lavenu and (for the German market) Breitkopf and Härtel. This appeared in print by October 1833 (as did a duet version of the Octet Op.20), several months before the orchestral parts. The full score was not published until March 1835. Mendelssohn refused a commission to produce a solo-piano transcription of the work, believing that the duet version could not be successfully reduced even further. However, much to the anger of Mendelssohn, Breitkopf and Härtel issued a solo version prepared by Friedrich Mockwitz (1773-1849) in 1834. Mendelssohn had nothing to do with this arrangement, though it is almost certain that Mockwitz's arrangement is derived from Mendelssohn's own four-hand transcription.

Initially, Mendelssohn had begun his *Scottish* Symphony in A minor Op. 56, in 1829, after spending several weeks touring Scotland. However, it was not until 1842 that the work was actually finished. The first performance took place in Leipzig, March 1842, another performance, in London, coming just three months later.

In a letter to his friend Karl Klingemann, in September 1842, Mendelssohn stated that the production of the duet arrangement required substantial amounts of time and energy. It was published by J. J. Ewer and Co., London and bore the title *Symphony, No. 3. Composed and Dedicated (by Permission) to Her Gracious Majesty Queen Victoria, by Felix Mendelssohn Bartholdy, Arranged as a Piano Forte Duett, By the Author. Op. 56.*

Mendelssohn's friendship with Queen Victoria and Prince Albert is well-documented. Less well-known is the fact that the composer made several unpublished arrangements of his music for the Royal Household. Below is the original manuscript of the end of *Frühlingslied*, from his *Lieder ohne Worte*, arranged for piano duet, now housed in the British Library.

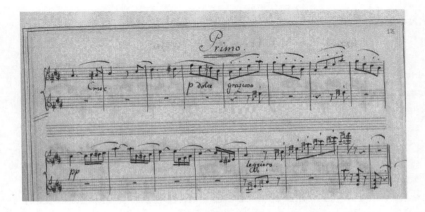

It is known that Mendelssohn arranged the second movement from the *Italian* Symphony in A Op. 90 for piano duet in 1834, a year after its first performance. He sent this to his sister, Fanny. However, the manuscript is now thought lost. The pair also performed a duet version of the Overture *Calm Sea and Prosperous Voyage* Op. 27.

Mendelssohn's reputation as a great composer was sealed with his composition of the oratorio *Elijah* Op. 70, first performed in Birmingham in 1846 and London in 1847 (the revised version). In England, Mendelssohn was seen as the natural successor to Handel, whose oratorios were extremely popular in early Victorian society.

Soon after the Birmingham performance, the publishers (Simrock in Germany and J. J. Ewer and Co. in England) were keen to receive Mendelssohn's completed (and revised) score as soon as possible. The director of Ewer and Company, Edward Buxton, wrote to Mendelssohn in November, 1846:

'There is moreover some danger in keeping the work too long out of print, as there is the possibility of some of the single pieces being copied out and getting into the hands of any of the music sellers here, who would be unprincipled enough to publish them before I could enrol my copyright, which I can only do when it is all in print. I know there are several looking out for it and who have expressed their determination to print the songs if they could get hold of them.'[36]

Mendelssohn sent the publishers the choral parts, orchestral parts and piano reduction for the vocal score in instalments from January 1847 onwards. Much to the annoyance of Edward Buxton, Mendelssohn made additional changes after he had sent them. On February 17, 1847, Mendelssohn wrote to Buxton:

'I am sorry to hear the no. 8 was already engraved, but I cannot help asking you not to mind these plates and to have it engraved, *as it stands here.* I assure you it is an improvement and must *stand* thus! And in order that you may not be too angry with me, I send today (via Simrock) the Overture a 4 mains and an Orchestra-Score of my Hymn, which I hope will reconcile you to the trouble you had for me and my alterations sake.'[37]

Thus, the duet version of the Overture was essentially a gift from Mendelssohn to his English publisher. It was not given to Simrock to publish. An additional reason for this being given as a gift was the fact that Mendelssohn had been unable to compose a more 'suitable' ending (as requested by Buxton) that would facilitate its performance as a concert overture and allow it to be sold as such.

Czerny transcribed several of Mendelssohn's works for piano duet. He sent Mendelssohn a copy of his arrangement of the Overture *Die Schöne Melusine* Op. 32, which was judged to be excellent. Czerny published approximately three hundred arrangements, based on themes from over one hundred different operas and ballets, plus symphonies, overtures and oratorios by such composers as, Auber (1782-1871), Bellini (1801-1835), Cherubini (1760-1842), Donizetti (1797-1848), Haydn, Meyerbeer (1791-1864), Mozart, Rossini (1792-1868), Spohr (1784-1859), Verdi, Wagner, Weber (1786-1826) as well as those already mentioned – Handel, Beethoven and Mendelssohn.

August Horn (1825-1893), who made numerous solo, duet and two piano transcriptions of major symphonic works by composers such as Beethoven, Bruch (1838-1920), Haydn, Mozart, Schubert and Schumann for Breitkopf and Härtel and later Peters, also arranged Mendelssohn's symphonies for eight hands. As mentioned earlier, the popularity of the eight-hand transcription was short-lived, the arrangements quickly going out of print.

In any discussion of the piano transcription, the first composer to spring to mind is undoubtedly Franz Liszt. The 'King of pianists', as Berlioz described him, gave thousands of concerts throughout Europe, playing a mixture of his own original works and the many transcriptions that he made. The reputation that he was the greatest pianist of all time was universally acknowledged by critics, composers and other virtuoso pianists alike. Composing some of the most technically demanding piano music ever written, Liszt became a living legend. A born showman, Liszt would appear in several different guises – the 'wild gypsy' one concert, the 'foppish dandy' the next. He composed well over 1300 works, edited many editions of music such as the Beethoven Sonatas and was an influential teacher, teaching over 400 prominent students across the years.

Surprisingly, Liszt composed a mere handful of completely original piano duets, with only one of these (the *Festpolonaise* of 1876) being of substance. A *Notturnu in E* and *Variation on Chopsticks* (a collaboration with Borodin (1833-1887), Cui (1835-1918), Rimsky-Korsakov and Liadov) are rather lightweight. However, his transcriptions for piano duet and two pianos were extensive – being a significant proportion of his transcriptions as a whole, numbering almost two hundred.

In a letter to his friend, Adolphe Pictet de Rochemont, in September 1837, Liszt clearly expressed his view of the relationship between the orchestra and piano:

'Within the span of its seven octaves it encompasses the audible range of the orchestra, and the ten fingers of a single person are enough to render the harmonies produced by the union of over a hundred concerted instruments... Thus it bears the same relation to an orchestral work that an engraving bears to a painting: it multiplies the original and makes it available to everyone, and even if it does not reproduce the colours, it at least reproduces the light and shadow'.[38]

David Wilde suggests that these transcriptions can be divided into two distinct groups:

'Lizst wrote one hundred and ninety-three transcriptions for the piano, of which forty-eight were re-arrangements of his own music; the rest were derived from a variety of different sources, from Bach to Wagner. They divide into two main types: *paraphrases*, in which the original work is transformed and freely re-composed, and *partitions*, in which Liszt faithfully transcribes a work from one medium to another, sometimes not deviating from the original by so much as a single note. The earliest example is of the first type, the *Fantasie sur la Tyrolìenne de l'Opera 'La Fiancée' par Auber* composed in 1829, when Liszt was eighteen. The last example is of the second type, a transcription of Cui's *Tarantella* which Liszt made in 1885, a year before his death.'[39]

A number of his transcriptions were, in fact, 'enlargements' rather than reductions i.e. he expanded the original solo piano texture when transcribing for duet or two pianos. The *Hungarian Rhapsodies* are excellent examples of this practice. Liszt transcribed the vast majority of his orchestral works too, including the twelve symphonic poems of the Weimar period (1848-61) - *Les Preludes*, *Mazeppa* and *Hamlet* being particularly well-known and the *Faust* and *Dante* Symphonies.

ASSEMBLY ROOMS, STAMFORD.

GRAND
MORNING CONCERT,
On Wednesday, Sept. 16, 1840,

To commence at 1 o'clock precisely.

M. LISZT,
First appearance this Season of this Extraordinary Pianist.

Mr. LAVENU, has the honor to inform the Nobility, Gentry and his
Friends, that he has succeeded in engaging

M. LISZT
Who will, on this occasion, perform his Grand Marche Hongroise, and
his Grand Galop Chromatique ; also a Grand Duet with

Mr. MORI.
Mr. RICHARDSON,
(The celebrated Flautist) will perform some of his most favorite Fantasias.

Mlle. DE VARNY,
Prima Donna of La Scala, Italian Opera, Paris, and Her Majesty's
Theatre, London, will sing some of her most popular Arias and Duos.

Miss LOUISA BASSANO
Of the Nobility's Concerts, will sing some of her admired Airs & Ballads

Mr. J. PARRY,
Will sing some of his latest and most admired Compositions.

Mr. LAVENU,
Will preside at the Piano Forte.

*Family Tickets, to admit four, 21s.—Single Tickets 6s. to be had
of Messrs. ROOE, MORTLOCK & JOHNSON.*

PROGRAMME.

PART 1.

TRIO—" L'usato ardir il mio," (Semiramide) Mlle. De
    Varny, Miss Bassano and Mr. J. Parry..*Rossini.*

ARIA—" Alfin son tua," (Lucia di Lammermoor)
    Miss Bassano ....*Donizetti.*

**MARCHE HONGROISE—Grand Piano
Forte—M. LISZT** ....*Liszt.*

DUETTO—" Sappi che un rio dovere,"(Bianca e Faliero)
    Mlle. De Varny and Miss Bassano ....*Rossini.*

BALLAD—"The Inchcape Bell," Mr. J. Parry ......*Parry.*

FANTASIA—Flute—Mr. Richardson.

ARIA—" L'Amor suo mi fe beato," (Roberto Devereux)
    Mlle De Varny ....*Donizetti.*

**FANTASIA ON FAVORITE AIRS—
Grand Piano Forte—M. LISZT** ......*Liszt.*

LYRIC LEGEND—" Ethelwige to Ethelred,"
    Miss Bassano ....*Wade.*

Mr. J. Parry will sing his new Song of " The Musical Husband."

PART 2.

DUETTO—" Colei Sofronio," (Torquato Tasso)
    Mlle. De Varny and Mr. J. Parry........*Donizetti.*

BALLAD—" Memory's Dream," Miss Bassano......*Lavenu.*

**GRAND DUETT—Piano forte—introducing
the favorite QUARTETT from Lucia di
Lammermoor, and GRAND GALOP
CHROMATIQUE, Messrs. LISZT and
MORI** ....*Liszt.*

ROMANCE—" I'm with thee." Mlle. De Varny ....*Wade.*

VARIATIONS—Flute—Mr. Richardson.

NEW DUETT—" The Sisters," Mlle. De Varny and
    Miss Bassano.

**MORCEAUX CHOISIS—from his cele-
brated Recitals, Piano Forte, M. LISZT**..*Liszt.*

SONG—"Wanted a Governess," Mr. J. Parry ......*Parry.*

TRIO—" Soave sia il vento," Mlle. De Varny.
    Miss Bassano and Mr. J. Parry............*Mozart.*

Conductor, Mr. LAVENU.

The Piano Forte is one of Erard's new patent, and is brought ex-
    pressly from London for the occasion.

An example of a concert given by Liszt, one in a series of fifty given
around England in 1840, promoted by the London impresario Lewis
Henry Lavenu. As well as playing solo, Liszt was joined by Lavenu's
half brother, Frank Mori, for the 'Grand Duett'.[40]

60

In a letter to Louis Köhler, dated 9 July 1856, Liszt suggested that he found the piano duet arrangements more restrictive than those for two pianos:

'the first seven numbers of the arrangements for two pianofortes of my Symphonic Poems have already appeared. An arrangement of that kind is not so easy to make use of as a four-hand one. Nevertheless, after I had tried to compress the score of *Tasso* plainly into one pianoforte, I soon gave up on this project for the others, on account of the unadvisable mutilation and defacement by the working into and through one another of the four-hand parts, and submitted to doing without tone and colour and orchestral light and shade, but at any rate fixing an abstract rendering of the musical contents which would be clear to the ear, by the two piano arrangement.'[41]

Liszt made four-hand arrangements of works by composers such as Beethoven, Bellini, Berlioz, Donizetti, Glinka (1804-1857), Meyerbeer, Mozart, Raff (1822-1882) and Schubert. He performed his arrangement of the *Symphonie Fantastique* Op. 14 extensively in an effort to promote the music of Berlioz. Liszt even paid for the transcription to be printed. Concerning the work, Liszt wrote: 'I have worked on this conscientiously as if I were transcribing Holy Scriptures, attempting to transfer to the piano not only the general structure of the music but all of its separate parts'. Liszt's advocacy certainly had the desired effect and Berlioz's music was to become highly regarded, with composers such as Balakirev (1837-1910), Chabrier (1841-1894), Czerny and Saint-Saëns (1835-1921) producing piano transcriptions. Berlioz himself never transcribed his orchestral work.

Liszt also sanctioned duet versions made by others mainly due to pressures of time, his own busy schedule and the sheer volume of work. In a letter to Friedrich Stade (1817-1902), the German organist, conductor and composer, Liszt wrote:

'If you will kindly take the trouble to arrange the entire *Faust* Symphony for two performers on one piano, I shall be greatly indebted to you. Deal as freely as possible with the figurations and also with the distribution among the seven octaves of the odious keyboard. It seems to me that what may be more literally accurate ought often to give way to what sounds better and even to what is convenient for the players at the piano.'[42]

This shows clearly that Liszt was thinking primarily in pianistic terms rather than being wholly intent on being as faithful to the original score as possible. This approach to transcription can be seen in many of his arrangements of the music of others and Liszt's arrangements of the Beethoven symphonies are, perhaps, a supreme example.

Beethoven – man and music – had a profound influence on Liszt. Whether or not the famous 'Weihekuss' (kiss of consecration) ever took place, it is clear that both men shared a mutual respect and admiration. Beethoven's music featured heavily in recital programmes given by Liszt and Liszt also conducted Beethoven symphonies with the Weimar Orchestra, raising funds for the proposed Beethoven statue at Bonn. Liszt possessed Beethoven's death mask, his Broadwood piano and even the original copy of Beethoven's will.

From the age of twenty-five, Liszt began the task of transcribing Beethoven's symphonies – a task which was to occupy him, on and off, for nearly thirty years. Liszt had a fascination with these works and his transcriptions were made (and published) in the full knowledge that there were already many existing arrangements competing in the market. Amongst the more notable, Kalkbrenner had completed a version of the entire cycle by 1840; Hummel had produced a set even earlier and Czerny, pupil of Beethoven, teacher of Liszt, had made the earliest transcriptions between 1827 and 1829. Liszt justified his actions in adding to the catalogue of arrangements in a preface to the Breitkopf and Härtel complete edition of the symphonies, published in 1865:

'the advances the piano has gained of late, in both the technique of performance and in mechanical improvement, make it possible to produce more and better arrangements than ever before. As a result of the vast development of its harmonic power, the piano is trying more and more to take possession of all orchestral compositions. Within the compass of its seven octaves it is capable, with but a few exceptions, of reproducing all the features, all the combinations, and all the configurations of the deepest musical creations. And it leaves to the orchestra no other advantages than those of contrasting tone colours and mass effects – immense advantages to be sure.

Such has been my aim in the work I lay before the public today. I confess that I should have to regard it as a rather useless employment of my time if I had produced just another version of the Symphonies in a manner up to now routine. But I shall think my time well spent if I have succeeded in transferring to the piano not only the grand outlines of Beethoven's compositions, but also that multitude of details and finer points that make such a significant contribution to the perfection as a whole.'

It is often assumed that, like the majority of Liszt's transcriptions, these were 'dashed off' with relative ease. However, as Alan Walker comments:

'Nothing could be further from the truth than to assume that Liszt took these transcriptions lightly, or that he threw them off with the same nonchalant ease that characterized much of his other output. On the contrary, they cost him a great deal of labor. They are the result of a profound study of the scores, of the keyboard, of the limitations of two hands, and of the art of transcription itself.'[43]

The music might be by Beethoven, but it is very much that of Liszt too. As Jim Samson has commented, it is in the transcriptions in particular that Liszt 'naturally and readily appropriated the thoughts of others and made them his own.'[44] Marc-André Roberge states that:

'Instead of simply transferring a work from one medium to another, Liszt knew how to translate it; in other words, he could grasp the essence, the *génie*, of the original and recreate it in pianistic terms, thereby respecting the essence of the new medium and making full use of its possibilities.'[45]

Beethoven's Fifth Symphony Op. 67 was — like today — one of his most popular works. Liszt was determined to produce a transcription that captured the fundamental essence of the work rather than simply reduce the work, note for note, for the keyboard. As already mentioned, Hummel's transcription (published by Schott) appeared several years before the one produced by Kalkbrenner (published by Schonenberger) and it is highly likely that Liszt had sight of both these. At the time these were highly rated. Comparing these two versions, and taking into account the fact that these are transcriptions and not original works, one is still somewhat struck by the huge similarities between the two (almost eighty percent of the bars are virtually identical). One might suspect that Kalkbrenner had Hummel's score to hand whilst drafting his own version. Liszt was impressed by neither.

The following is a comparative analysis of the First Movement 'Allegro con brio':

Introduction of the motto (bars 1 -21): Hummel and Kalkbrenner are virtually identical. Liszt immediately emphasises the dramatic opening by adding extra bass notes in the left hand (an octave below the orchestral score). Compared to both Hummel and Kalkbrenner, Liszt's part writing and division between hands is more logical and pianistic. At the end of this section, unlike Hummel and Kalkbrenner who follow the woodwind at the end of this section, Liszt follows the strings, thus writing an octave lower than the original.

Bars 22 — 58: Apart from the odd octave doubling or positioning of the notes within a chord, Hummel and Kalkbrenner are again identical. Liszt is not dissimilar until bar 37 when the left hand becomes more pronounced. At bar 44 he provides a simplified 'ossia' above a much more elaborate and pianistic passage where full chords in both hands move down in position.

Bars 59 – 124 (the horn introduces the second subject): The similarities between Hummel and Kalkbrenner continue – only occasional octave doublings indicate that these are entirely separate versions. Again, Liszt thinks more pianistically in his transcription. From bar 84, for example, he pedals through the bars, giving the chords a greater emphasis. The ending of this section is similar in all three versions, Liszt's chords being fuller and more spacious.

Bars 125 – 196 (start of the development): Neither Hummel or Kalkbrenner observe the pause at bar 128. However, in this section the Hummel and Kalkbrenner versions are less similar, with Kalkbrenner's being slightly more virtuostic with many octave doublings in the right hand. Hummel has some semiquaver split chords (bars 168 – 173). Liszt's transcription follows Kalkbrenner's reasonably closely, though towards the end of this section Liszt adds more pianistic touches such as the arpeggiated chords in bars 183 – 195. As is usual, Liszt's left hand is fuller and has a more prominent role.

Bars 197 – 248: In this section which includes minim chords (alternating between strings and woodwind in the original), all three transcriptions are lacking. Liszt thickens the chordal writing and emphasises the dramatic nature of the original music as the motto returns.

Bars 249 – end: Liszt announces the beginning of the recapitulation with *fff* chords, tremolo and the direction '8ᵃ bassa ad libitum'. Unlike Hummel and Kalkbrenner, Liszt is more adventurous as regards giving the left hand melody. A good example occurs at bars 323 – 330, where Liszt splits the theme between both hands. As the movement draws to a close, Liszt's transcription captures the raw energy of Beethoven's work, utilising a far greater range of notes than either Hummel or Kalkbrenner. Never deliberately 'showy', Liszt does introduce one of his trademark 'effects' from bar 415 – jumps in the right hand. Neither Hummel or Kalkbrenner are so daring!

Liszt's practice of performing in large concert halls to a massed audience drew criticism from Schumann in 'Neue Zeitschift für Musik', the weekly periodical he had founded in 1834. Denouncing Liszt's performance of Beethoven's *Pastoral* Symphony Op. 68, Schumann wrote:

'It was not a happy choice for many reasons. When performed at home in an intimate atmosphere, it is possible to forget the otherwise masterly and conscientiously made transcription from the orchestra. But in a large concert hall, in the same place where we have so often heard the symphony played perfectly by an orchestra, the lack of instrumentation stands out perceptibly, all the more so when the transcription vainly attempts to convey the orchestral mass in its full strength. A simpler arrangement, a mere intimation, would perhaps have far greater effect.'[46]

Liszt's popularity in the concert hall – particularly in England, rested upon, to a large extent, the transcriptions that he made. After studying with Franz Liszt in Rome in the 1860s, the English pianist Walter Bache (1842-88) returned to Britain, and organised a concert series from 1865-88 with one primary objective: to promote the music of his idol. Given the somewhat sporadic performances of Liszt's works in Britain following the composer's visit in 1840-41, these concerts were particularly significant in relation to the reception of Liszt's music in Britain. Bache initially relied upon the various transcriptions made by the composer. For example, the two piano transcription of *Les Préludes* was performed in 1869 as a preparation for the successful orchestral performances of 1871 and 1872. Previous to this, Bache had performed the duet version in 1865 with Edward

Dannreuther. *Mazeppa* in its two piano form was performed in October 1876, two months ahead of its British orchestral première at the Crystal Palace on 9 December 1876 and its second orchestral performance at Bache's concert in February 1877. One of Bache's final concerts was given on 21 January 1888 – the two piano version of Liszt's *Faust* Symphony. He was partnered by the then director of the London Symphony Concerts, Georg Henschel (1850-1934).

In his final years, Liszt continued to produce piano transcriptions at an astonishing rate. The last of these, made in 1885, just a year before his death, were piano duet transcriptions of the *Hungarian Rhapsodies* Nos. 18 and 19.

Brahms, Dvořák and Tchaikovsky

Johannes Brahms is undoubtedly the composer whose piano transcriptions of his own symphonic works are most widely known. However, the common view that Brahms simply transcribed his completed symphonies and other orchestral works for piano duet after completion is incorrect. The gestation of these works was much more complex.

Brahms began his first work for the Hamburg publisher Cranz — famous for publishing the work of the Strauss dynasty — in 1849, making piano arrangements under the pseudonym 'G. W. Marks'. Brahms made piano reductions of such works as *Les Huguenots* by Meyerbeer and Donizetti's *Lucia di Lammermoor* and *La Fille du Regiment*. His *Souvenir de la Russie — Transcriptions en forme de Fantaisies sur des Airs russes et bohémiens* Anh. IV/6 was given the spurious number Op. 151. It is one of Brahms's earliest pieces, dating from around 1850 and harks back to Brahms's early days as a tavern pianist on Hamburg's dockside. It was authenticated as the work of Brahms by Kurt Hofmann in 1971. In fact, several different composers working for Cranz used the name G. W. Marks. Brahms may well have produced other works and transcriptions as well, but nothing is clearly documented. Malcom Macdonald comments:

'Brahms's low opinion of his efforts in later years can probably be gauged from the fact that he was content to let them remain buried under a pseudonym. But they reveal a taste for the popular music of the day, and an interest in transcription, that remained with him throughout his life.' [47]

Brahms was fortunate to see the vast majority of his work appear in print and very much composed with eventual publication in his mind. Brahms usually adopted a three stage process when composing larger works.

One of the first piano duets composed by Brahms and authenticated as such in 1971.

Firstly, he would seek the opinion of close friends and colleagues — often playing the work as a piano duet. Secondly, he would carry out 'test' orchestral performances before any parts were published. Finally he would use his experience of conducting and hearing the score to make final corrections and revisions before committing the work to print.

Brahms's publisher, Simrock, keen to keep the composer happy, allowed Brahms the time he needed and employed one of their editors, Robert Keller, to act as proof-reader and assistant to Brahms, a job which he did for twenty years, from 1871 until his death. Not only did Keller manage to put into print the vast majority of Brahms's orchestral work, he also took on the less publicised role of producing piano transcriptions of some of Brahms's compositions. Initially, Brahms would scrutinise these carefully, making corrections and amendments but, as time went on, he was content for Simrock to issue these arrangements without any checking. Brahms and Keller corresponded mainly by letter and these have been archived in the Library of Congress and the Gesellschaft der Musikfreunde in Vienna and edited by George S. Bozarth.[48]

However, in the last few years of their associateship, Brahms grew increasingly frustrated by Keller's 'pedestrian' arrangements. Brahms felt that Keller included too much detail in his transcriptions. Rather than being too fussy, Brahms advocated an arrangement that was 'light, brisk, leaving out all that is possible just so it sounds really well for 4 hands and is playable!'[49] He began to champion Theodor Kirchner (1823-1903), composer, pianist and house arranger for Peters, but Simrock refused to dispense with the services of Keller.

Brahms made duet transcriptions of all his four symphonies, which were published by Simrock at more or less the same time as the full orchestral scores. Brahms often worked on the two versions simultaneously and would play through ideas to friends and colleagues on the piano, before deciding upon exact orchestration. For example, Clara Schumann (1819-1896) first heard the First Symphony in C minor Op. 68 in a solo piano arrangement performed by Brahms in the summer of 1876, several months before its orchestral première in November. She expressed disappointment initially, and it is hard to imagine, given their close relationship, that Brahms did not respond to her criticisms before completing the final version.

Clara and Robert Schumann. A number of Brahms' orchestral works were first heard on the piano in their home.

By June 1877, Brahms was working on the four-hand version of the First Symphony. He completed this by the end of the month and sent the score to Simrock. Further revisions were made throughout the summer to both the duet and full score – all carefully checked by Keller.

Unlike the First, which preoccupied Brahms for nearly fifteen years, the Second Symphony in D Op. 73 was composed in an intensive five-month period. Brahms completed the piano duet transcription in November 1877. Before its official première in Vienna, December 1877, three 'pre-rehearsals' were allocated – a 'Korrect-Probe' (proof-reading session), one full regular rehearsal plus a dress rehearsal. Before being printed, the work was also performed in Leipzig, Amsterdam, The Hague, Dresden and Düsseldorf. This work was a particular favourite of Brahms and he played the duet version a number of times with his friends.

71

The Third Symphony in F Op. 90 was given its first orchestral performance in 1883. Following this, Clara Schumann wrote to Brahms:

'I was furious when I heard that your F major symphony is now really going to appear arranged by [Robert] Keller. I think that it is very heartless of you, for no one can arrange your things half as well as you can yourself, and what a pleasure we shall all lose in consequence.'[50]

Brahms himself was not entirely happy with this situation. In October 1884 he wrote the following letter to Robert Keller:

'Dear Herr Keller,
I must request your kind attention!
Your arrangement is a most excellent proof of hard work, a token of devotion to and reverence for my piece. A great many aspects of it are praiseworthy – but – I just would have done it differently!
How often I have asked Herr Simrock not to send me arrangements for perusal and revision. I have my own particular views on arranging – my whims, if you wish, since most of today's good musicians will be on your side, not mine. I would in this case, as usual, have returned your arrangement without looking at it, had not a visitor recently enticed me to play it through. Now I cannot help but ask you and request that you tell me sincerely and honestly, without the *slightest misgiving*. May I rewrite the arrangement according to my taste? (This would affect mainly the 1st and 3rd movements, only slightly or not at all the 2nd and 4th).
My first stipulation is that this must not cause you any disadvantage at all, and also that the additional trouble not be for free.
You also may take no notice of my proposal and not inform Herr Simrock about this letter etc.
Herr Simrock indeed bears the blame, and I can promise, moreover, that the arrangement will be easier, more playable – and this will also sell better!

I simply treat my piece less respectfully, more audaciously than you or anyone else can.

In short, now and henceforth you can do whatever you wish, only do not misconstrue this inquiry, and perhaps write me a line.

Yours most sincerely,

J. Brahms.'[51]

Keller replied:

'....how could I object, if you are willing to take the trouble of rewriting my arrangement? I can only *welcome* the fact that you are willing to make your beautiful work available to a wider public in a piano arrangement that is in accordance with your intentions! I have told all of this to Herr Simrock as well, and have given him your letter to read, and he says that above all he wants to see you completely satisfied and that the not inconsiderable cost caused by a partial or even complete re-engraving will not prevent him from fulfilling your wishes.'[52]

Despite this assurance, Keller went on to produce several different transcriptions of the work – for piano duet, solo piano and two pianos, eight hands (all published by Simrock in 1884). The above letters reveal the beginnings of a strained relationship between the two men. A closer study of the language used suggests Brahms' less than enthusiastic support for Keller and, even more telling, Keller's response is laced with 'polite' sarcasm which would certainly not be lost on Brahms.

Brahms's Fourth Symphony Op. 98 was first performed on 25 October 1885 at Meiningen with the composer in charge. His publisher, Simrock was present at the performance. Previous to this, he had attempted to get agreement from Brahms to publish a four-hand transcription. However, Brahms himself was unsure about the work as a whole. On 2 October he had written to Simrock:

'I have no idea yet whether I shall have the thing published or not. Nevertheless, if I should go the way of all flesh, and therefore have no further voice in the matter, then the Symphony belongs to you; a present in Full Score and Piano arrangement, as it stands. For the present, however, I must think it over! It would be foolish for you to spend a penny on it! I am not in need of it, neither are my kith and kin, and as for a grave stone, or anything of that sort, I must tell you as plainly as I can that I don't care a pin for it!'[53]

Nevertheless, despite his initial doubts, the work received many more successful performances in the following months and was duly published the following year. Brahms made the four-hand transcription which he sent to the publisher on 2 November 1886 and Robert Keller was given the task of producing a solo piano arrangement.

Brahms also made piano duet transcriptions of many of his other orchestral works. *Ein Deutsches Requiem*, a self-contained reduction of the entire score (solo, choral and instrumental parts), has already been mentioned and there are transcriptions of the two *Serenades*, *Academic Festival Overture* (duet arrangement by Robert Keller with alterations by Brahms), and *Variations on a Theme by Haydn*. Of the many transcriptions made, Brahms assigned opus numbers to just two of them – the *Haydn Variations* Op. 56b and the Sonata for Two Pianos Op. 34b (a transcription of the Piano Quintet).

The Piano Concerto No. I Op. 15 (rejected by the publisher Breitkopf and Härtel) was subsequently published by the Swiss firm, Rieter-Biederman as a duet in 1864. The full score was not published until ten years later. Brahms took great care in producing the transcription. In a letter to the publisher dated February 11 1864 he wrote:

'I think I can pride myself on having made it practical and playable. . . .
The arrangement in question is meant to be performed and not, as is
the current fashion, sight-read.'[54]

Discussing the merits of this transcription, Ralph Neiweem and
Claire Aebersold state that:

'The passages of real interest are those in which soloist and orchestra
are playing together with full intensity. Here one might fear a
letdown; yet Brahms manages to condense the thunderous ending to
the first movement, for example – with its torrent of top-to-bottom
arpeggios for the soloist and stentorian melody for the orchestra – in
a manner that leaves nothing out except octave doublings, enabling
the players to be completely involved in projecting the emotional
excitement of the moment. Brahms achieves his results in these
sections by emphasizing contrapuntal clarity and complexity over
harmonic coloration.'[55]

On the subject of the *Haydn Variations*, Michael Musgrave confirms
the view that Brahms did not simply transcribe his orchestral works
once complete:

'Although more familiar in their orchestral version, the Haydn
Variations seem to have been conceived in both forms simultaneously
and the two piano version may rightly be taken as a culmination in
relation to its keyboard predecessors.'[56]

There is little doubt that Brahms enjoyed the task of producing
transcriptions. After completing the piano duet reduction of the
Serenade No. 2 in A Op. 16, (one of his earliest orchestral
compositions) Brahms wrote to Joachim:

'These days I have arranged my second serenade for four hands. Don't
laugh! It gives me great pleasure. I have seldom written music with
greater delight; it seemed to sound so beautiful that I was overjoyed. I

can honestly say that my happiness was not increased by the knowledge that I was the composer. But it was amusing, all the same.'[57]

Brahms and Keller transcribed several of the chamber works for piano duet too – the String Quartets, String Quintets, String Sextets and Piano Quartets.

Towards the end of his life, Brahms decided to make two piano transcriptions of his symphonies, starting with the Third and Fourth. He offered to produce similar versions of the first two but discovered that Keller had already undertaken this task. Initially displeased, he ordered Simrock to send him copies for checking. To his surprise, he found them to be far better than expected. In May 1890 he wrote:

'I am rather pleased I had the arrangement by Keller sent to me; I had no displeasure in it, but genuine joy. Not only are they set in a touchingly diligent manner, but they are also pleasing to the ear and skilfully done. My fingers would rather play differently – but otherwise I have nothing to desire and alter in his very good work.'[58]

Brahms at the piano towards the end of his life.

Brahms had a particularly important part to play in the elevation of Dvořák, from semi-successful provincial musician to world-class composer. Significantly, it was a piano duet that secured his international reputation, the *Slavonic Dances* Op. 46, published in 1878.

Dvorák had struggled for years to be a composer before becoming, quite literally, an overnight success. A rank-and-file orchestral player, he wrote what he could in what little spare time he had available, in between concerts, rehearsals and teaching – his main source of income until 1878. He won the Austrian State Stipendium (a grant newly created by the Ministry of Education to assist 'young, poor and gifted' musicians) in 1874, and again in 1876 and 1877. The influential Viennese music critic, Eduard Hanslick (1825-1904), was a jury member and approved of Dvorák's music. He encouraged Brahms, another Stipendium judge, to use his influence to promote Dvorák as a composer.

Brahms recommended Dvorák to his publisher, Simrock, who published the *Moravian Duets* Op. 32, the success of these leading to the commissioning of the *Slavonic Dances* Op. 46, written between March and May 1878, for piano duet. A huge success throughout Europe, the initial print run ran out in a matter of a couple of days. In their version for piano duet, they became one of the most profitable works ever published by Simrock. Maximising this success, Simrock also issued several chamber works by Dvorák in the same year. The publisher Bote and Bock also published some of Dvorák's work.

Like a number of other original piano duets, such as *Legends* Op. 59, *From the Bohemian Forest* Op. 68 and another set of *Slavonic Dances* Op. 72, Dvorák orchestrated these later on. Conversely, he produced duet transcriptions of his orchestral works. The Sixth Symphony Op. 60 was the first to be published and Simrock numbered it No.1. It was dedicated to the famous conductor of the Vienna Philharmonic, Hans Richter (1843-1916). It is said that in a private reading of the work given by Dvorák on the piano, Richter hugged Dvorák at the conclusion of each movement. The piano duet version, also published by Simrock, contains no number. So popular was this work that the Philharmonic Society in London immediately asked for another. Simrock published the Seventh Symphony Op. 70 as No.2 and the Fifth Op. 76 as No.3.

The duet transcription of the Ninth Symphony *From the New World* Op. 95 is the most well-known, having received several recordings and is worth looking at in close detail:

The transcription is almost entirely faithful to the orchestral score with, for example, the dynamics of the original reproduced exactly (even if these may be impossible to reproduce on the piano e.g. tied notes originally played on the horn are also marked *fz > pp*). As a general texture, Dvořák has the secondo playing string parts, the primo the brass and woodwind, though this varies to some extent throughout the work. Also of interest, the secondo appears to be more demanding technically than the primo – this may be, in all probability, deliberate, with Dvořák having an eye for the domestic market where one player might prefer the 'easier' part.

In the primo part, there are numerous occasions where Dvořák moves the woodwind parts up an octave (often then doubled by the left hand playing at the original pitch). This gives the melodic line greater prominence and is usually done not for reasons of logistics alone. Similarly, but less often, Dvořák has the secondo playing an octave lower than the double bass – an attempt to create the fullest of sounds on the piano. In the final movement, Dvořák includes the second to lowest note on the keyboard – a very rare example of this particular 'b' being notated. Additional markings appear in the duet arrangement – again an attempt to give a melodic line an extra importance e.g. *express* for the flute solo at bar 149, *dolce* for the violin melody at bar 157, *marc.* for the trumpet call at bar 184 (all first movement).

Only very occasionally does Dvořák include additional material in the piano reduction. This is usually to make the piano writing flow better especially in semiquaver passages. Once or twice he leaves out some top woodwind parts when the upper string writing takes precedence. In the third movement (Fig 5), Dvořák adds additional top notes and jumps in the octave to suggest the interplay between flute and violin.

In studying the full orchestral score, one realises just how often Dvořák uses tremolando effects in the strings. These are replicated in the piano transcription – perhaps rather too often as this can be rather tiresome when listening. In the second movement (Fig. 2) the piano writing becomes particularly complex with Dvořák writing out the tremolandos in both secondo and primo parts in an attempt to match the original as closely as possible.

Composed in 1875, Dvořák's nationalistic opera *Vanda* Op. 25, was sold to the publisher August Cranz in 1881. A piano duet version of the Overture was first published in 1884, the full orchestral score not published until 1900. Dvořák's autograph score was destroyed in Allied bombing on Leipzig during the Second World War.

 **Dvořák, pictured at the time of his writing the Ninth Symphony.**

Brahms also had a profound influence on the English composer Charles Villiers Stanford (1852-1924). His Third *Irish* Symphony Op. 28 was written after hearing the English première of Brahms's Fourth Symphony and was closely modelled on it. Stanford received great critical success for this work and it was programmed in numerous concerts. As late as 1911, Mahler took up the work and conducted it with the New York Philharmonic. In an effort to popularise the work, Stanford's publisher, Novello, as well as issuing the full score, published a piano duet transcription made by Charles Wood (1866-1926), English composer and pupil of Stanford at the Royal College of Music.

Although virtually unknown today, there exist piano duet versions of all of Tchaikovsky's symphonies. In his many letters, Tchaikovsky wrote in detail about his compositions and the processes involved in their creation. Additionally, he wrote numerous notes on his scores giving an indication of when and where they had been composed. Tchaikovsky was always aware of the value of piano transcriptions in spreading awareness and knowledge of his compositions to the wider public.

Tchaikovsky's First Symphony *Winter Daydreams* Op. 13 was begun in 1866 and revised in 1874. Initially, only the Adagio and Scherzo were approved for performance in the Russian Musical Society concert series (on 10 December 1866), a full performance not taking place until a year later (February 1868). As well as publishing the full score in 1875, Jurgenson commissioned Eduard L. Langer (1835-1905), a pianist and teacher at the Moscow Conservatory, to make a piano duet transcription. Tchaikovsky personally checked this but stated that 'the arrangement was made very badly and printed with dozens of careless mistakes.'

Tchaikovsky's Second Symphony *Little Russian* Op. 17 was composed in 1872 and revised 1879-1880. It was first performed 26 January 1873 to great critical acclaim. Subsequently, V.V. Bessel offered to print the work and produce a four-hand version. On this matter, Tchaikovsky wrote to Bessel:

'Regarding the symphony, I believe it would be best if Mme Korsakova took it upon herself to make the arrangement. With the exception of Laroche, I cannot think of anyone else who could do this well, apart from myself. I dislike this work, but in extreme circumstances I would do it myself, so long as you don't want me to finish it all by the summer.'[59]

Tchaikovsky's recommendation probably sprang from the fact that at an informal gathering of musicians at the home of Rimsky-Korsakov,

Mme Korsakova had expressed a wish to arrange the symphony. Tchaikovsky stated that 'she begged me in tears to let her arrange it for four hands.'[60] Mme Korsakova (formerly Nadezhda Nikolayevich Purgold 1848-1919) was renowned for her expertise in the art of transcribing symphonic works for piano duet. Her arrangements of Tchaikovsky's *Romeo and Juliet* and several works of her husband such as the tone poem *Sadko* Op.5 and the *Antar* Symphony Op.9 are particularly notable. Indeed, her transcriptions are viewed far more favourably than those made by her husband. Rimsky-Korsakov himself arranged the *Capriccio Espagnol* Op.32 and *Scheherazade* Op.35 for piano duet. The transcription of the latter took just two weeks to prepare in the spring of 1889.

Nadezhda Purgold.

However, due to ill health, Mme Korsakova was unable to start the task and Tchaikovsky decided to produce the transcription himself. He completed the first movement by the end of May 1873. He sent this to Mme Korsakova so that she could review the arrangement and make any necessary amendments. Tchaikovsky then abandoned the project, passing the work on to Nikolai A. Hubert (1840-1888). Hubert had been a close friend of Tchaikovsky since their days together at the St. Petersburg Conservatory. Hubert completed the task in approximately four months, passing the arrangement back to Tchaikovsky for a final check before being published (November 1873). However, the full score remained unpublished at this time.

When revising the work between December 1879 and January 1880, Tchaikovsky wrote to his patron, Nadezhda von Meck:

'I am engaged in reviewing the symphony and have found parts of it to be so poor that I have made up my mind to rewrite the first and third movements, to alter the second, and just to shorten the last. And so if all goes well in Rome, I should turn this immature and mediocre symphony into a good one.'[61]

Tchaikovsky's ability to work quickly was, at times, capricious. He completed almost half of the re-worked first movement in a matter of a day. Whilst engaged in the copying process, he made a completely new piano duet version. V.V. Bessel finally published the full score, orchestral parts and the new piano duet version in 1881.

The creation of the Third Symphony Op. 29 in D major was relatively straight-forward as compared to the first two symphonies. Composed in a three month period (June-August 1875), it was first performed in Moscow (7 November 1875) followed by its St. Petersburg première on 24 January 1876. Jurgenson issued the orchestral parts in December 1876, the full score in January 1877 and in April, the piano duet version. This was again produced by E.L Langer. Langer also transcribed selections from *Swan Lake* Op. 20 and produced an eight-hand arrangement of the *Capriccio Italien* Op. 45.

Following quickly on from the Third Symphony, the Fourth in F minor Op. 36 (composed between March and December 1877) was first performed in Moscow 10 February 1878. Tchaikovsky urged Jurgenson to entrust the duet arrangement to either Sergei Taneyev (1856-1915) or Karl Klindworth (1830-1916), piano professor at the Moscow Conservatory — 'There are but two men in Moscow — nay, in the whole world — to whom I would entrust the arrangement of my symphony for four hands.'[62] He also contacted Taneyev directly with his request, which Taneyev agreed to.

A Monsieur Ch. Davidoff.

Capriccio Italien

pour

grand Orchestre

composé par

P. Tschaikowsky.

OP. 45.

Partition d'orchestre Pr. M. 10.50 net.
Parties d'orchestre Pr. M. 27. net.
(VI. II. Va. à. M. 1.50, Ve.et Basse. M 2.10 net)
Arrangement pour petit Orchestre par Fritz Hoffmann.
Partie de conducteur. Pr. M. 3. net.
Parties d'orchestre Pr. M. 15. net.
(VI. II. Va. à. M. 1.50, Ve. et Basse .M 2.10 net)
Arrangement pour Orchestre militaire par Carl Eilhardt.
Partition d'orchestre Pr. M. 9. net.
Parties d'orchestre Pr. M 21. net.
Pour Piano à 2 mains par H. Pachulski Pr. M 5.
Pour Piano à 4 mains par l. Auteur Pr. M 6.
Pour 2 Pianos à 8 mains par E. Langer Pr. M 10.

Propriété de l'Éditeur.
Enregistré aux Archives de l'Union.
Gr Méd. d'or

D. RAHTER,
HAMBURG & LEIPZIG.
Moscou, P. Jurgenson.   Paris, Mackar & Noël.

Inst. Lith. de C.G. Röder Leipzig

The *Capriccio Italien* was arranged for small orchestra by Fritz Hoffmann, for military band by Carl Eilhardt, for solo piano by H. Pachulski, for eight hands by E. Langer and for piano duet by Tchaikovsky himself. Like Tchaikovsky, Henryk Pachulski (1859-1921) also benefitted from the patronage of Nadezhda von Meck.

83

Taneyev was a composition student of Tchaikovsky at the Moscow Conservatory and gave the première performance of the solo part of the First Piano Concerto Op. 23 and the first performances of several other piano works. In June 1879, Tchaikovsky checked the piano arrangement and this was printed the following August. The full score appeared a year later.

The initial idea for the *Manfred* Symphony in B minor Op. 58 came from Balakirev who sent Tchaikovsky a detailed programme for each movement, suggesting that he study Berlioz's *Symphonie Fantastique* Op. 14 and *Harold* Op. 16.

Whilst orchestrating the symphony, Tchaikovsky simultaneously made his own arrangement for piano duet. Concerned that it might be rather too difficult to play, he sent it to Alexandra I. Hubert (formerly Alexandra Batalina 1850-1937), the wife of N.A. Hubert who had worked on the Second Symphony. She was a talented pianist and one of Tchaikovsky's closest female friends who arranged several other Tchaikovsky works including *Eugene Onegin* Op. 24, the *Slavonic March* Op. 31 and the First and Third String Quartets. She sent back her own version to Tchaikovsky who, in turn, corrected and adapted the arrangement. Tchaikovsky then sent this on to Balakirev who may have had some input as well.

The work was first performed in March 1886 a month after its full score publication by Jurgenson. In April that year, the piano duet transcription appeared with both Tchaikovsky and Alexandria Hubert credited. Rachmaninov is also known to have produced a version of *Manfred* for piano duet but the manuscript is lost.

The Fifth Symphony in E minor Op. 64 was composed between May and August 1888. Tchaikovsky returned to Taneyev to complete the transcription. So keen was he to aid Taneyev in this process, that he sent him each movement as it was completed. Both the full score and the piano duet arrangement were published simultaneously by

Jurgenson before the end of the year. Taneyev and A.I. Ziloti performed part of the Symphony in October 1888 at a concert for the Russian Nobles Society before the orchestral première in St. Petersburg (5 November 1888).

Tchaikovsky's last and most feted symphony, the *Pathetique* in B minor Op. 74, like most of the others, was composed in a relatively short period of seven months (from February to August 1893). As was the case with the *Manfred* Symphony, Tchaikovsky worked simultaneously on a piano duet transcription whilst scoring the work. Following a short period of rest, Tchaikovsky returned to the Symphony in October, making revisions to both the full score and the reduction. He arranged for the violinist, Jules Konyus (1869-1942) to advise him on bowings and for his brother, Lev Konyus (1871-1944) to look over the piano arrangement, allowing him to make certain alterations, as necessary. Jules, having heard Tchaikovsky play at the piano, commented:

'I must confess that I was really not in the least attracted by the actual music of the Sixth Symphony since the author's performance was as bad as one may imagine. His red hands with thick and by no means supple fingers pounded out the most poignant passages crudely and hurriedly, as if they hastened to finish and rid themselves of that boring thing.'[63]

Lev Konyus and Taneyev performed the duet at a concert held at Taneyev's house on 20 October 1893. Ippolitov-Ivanov who was present noted that 'the symphony did not make much impression on us.'[64]

The first official performance came in October 1893 at St. Petersburg (again as part of the Russian Musical Society concert series) though there may have been an earlier one performed by the students of the Moscow Conservatory several weeks previous to this, in order to facilitate the correction of orchestral parts. By the time of these performances, Jurgenson had already published the full score. Sadly, Tchaikovsky died just a few months before the duet arrangement was published in February 1894.

Pyotr Ivanovich Jurgenson (1836-1904) - friend and publisher of Tchaikovsky. He commissioned the young composer to produce several duet arrangements of orchestral works by composers such as Rubenstein and Meyerbeer and maintained a life-long associateship with him.

Tchaikovsky had written to his nephew Vladimir Davidov in February 1893, commenting that the symphony was programmatic in nature, 'profoundly subjective' and was to remain 'an enigma to all.' From its very opening, a sense of darkness – perhaps despair – looms over the work. Whether or not the work reveals anything about Tchaikovsky's inner self (his homosexuality produced extreme feelings of guilt and self-hatred) is the topic of much speculation. Certainly, the composer's death so soon after its first performance and the mystery surrounding it, adds fuel to the argument.

The opening Adagio is, perhaps, the least successful section of the work in its piano duet format, the piano struggling to convey the brooding sonorities of the lower strings and bassoon, so important in establishing the work's character. At the *Allegro non troppo*, the interaction between strings and woodwind is lost but Tchaikovsky remains entirely faithful to the orchestral score when transcribing, both in terms of pitch and a gradual building up of the texture. For the majority of the movement, the primo part fuses the woodwind, horn and upper string parts with the secondo carrying the lower parts. At times, Tchaikovsky's desire to maintain exact pitch relations results in what might be termed a 'degradation' of the sound i.e. high flute and piccolo parts transferred to the top end of the keyboard sound almost comedic rather than incisive.

For the most part, Tchaikovsky maintains in the transcription the surging rhythms of the original. Only occasionally does he make compromises. For example, the viola figure (bars 21-22) is made more playable on the piano by missing out one of the three repeated notes which occur every beat and the ascending string septuplet figure (bar 108) is played only in part to facilitate the playing of the flute/oboe melody at the start of the bar. The lyrical second subject fares well in the transcription, being more chordally based, especially so when accompanied by triplets (from bar 130 onwards). Dynamically, Tchaikovsky includes the vast majority of the original markings. All the *pppp* markings are included but not the *pppppp* at bar 160 – possibly the quietest notes a composer has ever called for.

The second and third movements are the most successful parts of the transcription. In the *Allegro con grazia* (a 5/4 rhythm often referred to as being disguised as a waltz), the secondo part has the more important role, reproducing the lyrical cello theme at the start, the primo taking over at the entry of the woodwind. The delicate string octave jumps sound well on the piano (bars 26-29). Tchaikovsky even asks the primo player to play *quasi pizzicato* (bar 34) in order to evoke the string writing. Of interest is the marking at orchestral point D *con dolcezza e flebile.* In the piano transcription this is replaced by *sempre mf in la mano sinistra* – perhaps an attempt by Tchaikovsky to convey the mood required which would normally be evident, to a large extent, by orchestral timbre.

Avoiding a conventional scherzo, Tchaikovsky composed a brilliant march for the third movement. Perhaps even more successful than the previous movement in its translation to piano duet, the transcription captures the mood of the music almost in its entirety, from the opening *moto perpetuo* 'chattering' strings, deft woodwind figurations to the gradual building up of texture and the emergence of the march theme (which Tchaikovsky gives to all four hands at various points in the movement). In the orchestral version, Tchaikovsky's magnificent orchestral palette is very much to the fore, and although the piano timbre cannot match this, the sheer exuberance of the music carries the transcription to a gripping climax with dazzling virtuoso piano writing.

Like the first movement, the final movement, imbued with despair, the slow descending melodic lines reminding us of the inevitability of death, does not translate successfully to the medium of the piano duet. The almost chorale-like section (bar 39 onwards) marked *con lenezza e devozione* works reasonably well, as does the gradual build up which follows. However, the final section, where brass sonorities are so important – the deep, mournful tuba, the rasping horns, is, one has to admit, a mere shadow of the original in its transcribed form.

Like Brahms, Tchaikovsky viewed piano reductions of his orchestral work as important musical documents in their own right. Unlike Brahms, however, Tchaikovsky did not take any great pleasure in their production. Thus, some of the work was passed on to others as circumstances arose – mostly friends and colleagues of the composer. Tchaikovsky – ever the perfectionist and always intensely concerned about his reputation – scrutinised these in minute detail to ensure that the transcriptions met his exacting standards. Therefore, to state that these transcriptions reflect the intentions and wishes of Tchaikovsky himself, is more than simple conjecture.

Bruckner and Mahler

Bruckner's work received both criticism and praise in equal proportions throughout his lifetime. As an organist and teacher he was well respected but his orchestral works were often derided. In 1868, at the age of 44, he joined the staff of the Vienna Conservatory. Here, he concentrated on writing symphonies but had his early efforts rejected by the Vienna Philharmonic Orchestra. Symphony No. 1 was described as 'wild', Symphony No. 2 as 'nonsense' and Symphony No. 3 as 'unplayable'.

Thus, the first notable performances of the early symphonies were transcriptions for either solo piano or piano duet and their importance cannot be underestimated. They were mostly performed at Vienna Academic Wagner Society meetings (so-called 'internal evenings') held at the Bösendorfer Hall. Many of Bruckner's pupils belonged to the Society and apart from Wagner's work, the Society also promoted the music of other composers such as Liszt and Wolf (1860-1903) as well as Bruckner. The transcriptions were produced by a number of different individuals — most of whom were students and friends of Bruckner and part of his 'Gaudeamus' inner-circle.

Great composers have always attracted admirers and the usual 'hangers-on'. However, Bruckner had more than his fair share of the latter and their collective influence upon his work is still very much an area that has to be fully explored. Three of the most influential figures in Bruckner's life and output were Ferdinand Löwe (1865-1925), Josef Schalk (1857-1901) and his younger brother Franz (1863-1931).

Löwe was a brilliant pianist and performed his own transcription of the Adagio from Bruckner's Second Symphony at his first professional concert in 1884. As a conductor, he was a leading figure in promoting Bruckner's orchestral works. He produced a piano duet transcription of the Fourth Symphony in 1890 (later revised by Josef Venantius von Wöss (1863-1943) and published by Universal Edition in 1927).[65] Joseph Schalk acted as Bruckner's chief piano arranger and was nick-named 'Generalissimus' by Bruckner — an indication, almost certainly, of the relationship the two men had. Criticism has been levelled at all three men, the Schalk brothers in particular, for making alterations to Bruckner's work. These range from relatively small textural changes to large-scale editing of the symphonic works.

Bruckner, whose admiration of Wagner almost verged on sycophancy, was desperate to win his approval. He visited Wagner at Bayreuth in September 1873, presenting him with both the Second and Third Symphonies, eager to gain Wagner's personal permission for a dedication. Wagner preferred the Third and afterwards, Bruckner referred to this work as his *Wagner* Symphony.

Although initially composed between 1872-73, revised twice in 1874 and 1876, it was not until December 16, 1877 that Bruckner finally conducted the première of his Third Symphony in the Musikverein Concert Hall, Vienna, for the Gesellschaft der Musikfreunde (Society for the Friends of Music). The work was deemed to be a failure but amongst the few individuals that did not express vocal contempt or leave the concert early, was a young and impressionable Mahler. The work made such an impact that he subsequently transcribed it for piano duet (movements one to three) along with Rudolph Krzyzanowski (1862-1911), fellow student of Mahler, who arranged the last movement. This version was published, alongside the full score, by Theodor Rattig, a partner in the publishing firm of Bussjager and Rattig, at his own expense. He had attended the performance of the symphony as well as all the rehearsals.

The first Bruckner symphony to be published, the transcription was also, significantly, Mahler's first publication in 1880. Mahler and Krzyzanowski played the transcription to Karl Goldmark (1830-

1915), one of the founders of the Wagner Society and Joseph Schalk at the Vienna Academy. Later, Mahler is known to have performed the duet with the Director of the Peters publishing firm, Henri Hinrichsen. Mahler championed Bruckner's work throughout his life, conducting the Fourth, Fifth and Sixth Symphonies in Vienna (1899-1901) and the whole cycle in New York in 1908.

The first public performance of Mahler's arrangement was given by Hans Paumgartner (1844-1896) and Felix Mottl (1856-1911) on 12 November 1879 at the Bösendorfer Hall, Vienna. On 4 February 1880 they were to perform the second and third movements of the Fourth Symphony in the presence of Bruckner and played the first movement on 7 October, later that year. This was the first ever performance of the work and they played it again the following year, perhaps in preparation for the orchestral performance which took place in March 1881.

Bruckner, a man riddled with self-doubt and suffering from periods of mental instability, took any criticism to heart. Unfortunately, one of the most influential and feared critics, Eduard Hanslick, disliked Bruckner's music intensely and went as far as trying to prevent Bruckner attaining a lectureship at the University of Vienna. He continually questioned Bruckner's abilities as a composer. Each following symphony was attacked. This, in turn, encouraged Bruckner into making numerous revisions to his work – all geared towards making his symphonies more acceptable to both audiences and critics. Deryck Cooke commented:

'The textural problem presented by the different versions of Bruckner's symphonies is one of the most vexatious in all musicology, and the person ultimately responsible is Bruckner himself. Had he only possessed the normal self-confidence of the great composer, he would have produced, like Beethoven or Dvorák, a single definitive score of each of his nine symphonies.'[66]

Bruckner would play his compositions on the piano to anyone who would care to listen.

In February 1875, Bruckner began work on his Fifth Symphony, completing it by May 1876. As mentioned previously, Bruckner was never to hear the work, apart from in a two piano transcription prepared by Joseph Schalk, performed in Vienna on 20 April 1887 by Joseph Schalk and Franz Zottman. Even at this stage, Bruckner was worried about the reception the work would have. Before the performance he wrote to Schalk requesting that he perform something else. Schalk wrote back saying that he had invested too much time on the work to not perform it and that Bruckner should not worry about the critics. Bruckner insisted that he attend rehearsals before the arrangement was heard in public. According to Friedrich Klose (1862-1942), another member of the 'Gaudeamus', Bruckner was ill-tempered throughout the rehearsal period:

'Bruckner was resolved to find fault with everything. He sat in the front row, the score on his knee, and interrupted continually, complaining that a thematic inner part wasn't strong enough, or that he couldn't hear this or that figuration, the next minute declaring that no one could make out the contrapuntal lines when the playing was so ill-defined; and then the forte passages weren't loud enough, even though the players were at the end of their strength and their fingers were almost bleeding from the effort.'[67]

At the actual concert itself, Bruckner sat nervously throughout, until the end of the final movement was greeted with a huge cheer and applause. Bruckner began to smile, bowed to the audience and treated everyone to 'the best wine'.

Bruckner's pupils continued to champion his work. They saw him as the natural heir to Beethoven, a Wagnerian symphonist in opposition to Brahms. Michael Steinberg comments:

'They believed that the only thing wrong with Bruckner's symphonies was that they were not Wagnerian enough. They cut and restitched, they imposed a Wagnerian ebb and flow on Bruckner's sense of pace and changed the orchestration from the unfussy magnificence of the originals to a Wagnerian impasto.'[68]

In February 1884, Joseph and Franz Schalk presented the Seventh Symphony in a piano duet version jointly made by themselves to the Leipzig Kapellmeister, Artur Nikisch (1855-1922), in an attempt to win him over and arrange a full performance. This he did in December 1884 at the Leipzig Gewandhaus. Another performance came in Munich three months later. Despite Hanslick's comment that the work was 'unnatural, self-important, morbid and twisted', this Seventh Symphony was greatly acclaimed and Bruckner was finally given due recognition as a great composer.

Surprisingly, given the reputation of the Schalks, the piano transcription remains entirely faithful to the published score as edited by Leopold Nowak (1904-1991). It was originally published by A. J. Gutmann in 1896 (the copyright was later transferred to Universal Edition). There is no deviation from the orchestral material whatsoever, with each bar of the reduction matching that of the original. This is, of course, partly explained by the fact that the Seventh Symphony is the least problematic of the symphonic works as regards differing versions – only Bruckner's autograph manuscript survives. Extremely well-written, containing a number of virtuoso passages, the transcription is nevertheless playable by a pair of very good amateur pianists. It is particularly important for including precise tempo indications and a number of expression markings which do not appear in the published orchestral version. There are also several instances of a slowing down being indicated followed by a return to the original tempo which is missing from the orchestral score. The transcription gives us a clear indication as to how the work was performed in Bruckner's time and it is very probable that Bruckner would have been consulted on (or perhaps suggested) these tempo indications and other markings. This arrangement is currently in the Kalmus catalogue and spuriously claims to be the composer's own transcription. A two piano version appeared in 1890, transcribed by Hermann Behn (1857-1927). Another member of Bruckner's inner circle, Cyrill Hynais (1867-1913) – again a pupil of the composer, who acted as Bruckner's copyist in his last years and edited the posthumous publication of the Sixth Symphony, made a solo piano transcription of the work in 1895.

With the increasing recognition and success of Bruckner's work, Löwe turned his attention to the First Symphony – a work which had received only one performance in Linz back in 1868. On 22 December 1884, Löwe and Josef Schalk performed the work and repeated this the following year on 23 April.

On 22 November 1892 Josef Schalk performed a solo piano transcription of the Eighth Symphony. Critics were united in their belief that two hands did not do justice to the work and that a four-hand arrangement was needed at the very least.

Löwe performed a solo transcription of the first movement of the Sixth Symphony (a first performance as the Vienna Philharmonic had only performed the second and third movements in 1883).

After Bruckner's death in 1896, Josef Schalk and Löwe collaborated on a duet transcription of the Ninth Symphony, published by Doblinger in 1903, two years after the death of Schalk. This work is, in many ways, a culmination of all that had gone before. Like Tchaikovsky's final Symphony, the work is associated with death, but, unlike that of Tchaikovsky, Bruckner's 'death' results in a glorious ascension rather than a gradual decline and acceptance of the inevitable. Perhaps more than most, the piano transcription is a mere recalling of the notes, unable to capture the uplifting experience (some may even consider this to be semi-religious) of listening to the orchestral version. Following this, complete cycles of the symphonies arranged for piano were published by C. F. Peters – Karl Grunsky (1871-1943), leading scholar, critic and great supporter of both Bruckner and Wagner, produced two piano versions and Otto Singer transcribed the works for piano duet.

Franz Schalk – his influence over Bruckner is well documented but the extent of the changes he made to Bruckner's symphonic output has yet to be fully established.

Bruckner bequeathed the autograph manuscripts of his symphonies to the Imperial Library in Vienna with the specific instruction that they should be made available to the publisher Josef Eberle for publication. However, it was not until the 1930's that a complete critical edition of Bruckner's works was begun, under the directorship of Robert Haas (1886-1960) up until the outbreak of the Second World War and then Leopold Nowak from 1945. However, there is no general agreement as to whether the Haas or the Nowak editions are the most accurate. Whilst it has been the case that the Nowak editions have been favoured more recently, the editions produced by Haas are now undergoing a revival, with several leading conductors declaring them to be the more preferable – but not necessarily the most authentic.

There are many contemporary accounts of Bruckner playing extracts from his symphonies on the piano to colleagues and friends. Anton

Meissner (1855-1932), a student of Bruckner, recounted how the composer would play to him and seek his opinion:

'Having greeted me, he would take out the piece of notepaper which accompanied him everywhere, walk over to the wretched, out-of-tune piano and play me excerpts from the *Te Deum* and the Seventh Symphony, which he was working on at the time. He would then ask me which particular version he should choose. He tried out this experiment with many people.'[69]

Although Bruckner did not make his own reductions, playing the piano using either a full score, notebook or, more commonly, playing from memory, it is almost certain that his playing influenced those who actually made the transcriptions. Conversely, it is also almost certain that Bruckner himself would have had some hand in their production – such was his method of working with his students.

The many duet performances were a key element in promoting the Bruckner 'cause'. Perhaps, more than any other nineteenth century composer, the key to understanding Bruckner's works is repeated listening. These concerts allowed the public to become familiar with the music in the absence of orchestral performances. In this respect, we should acknowledge the important work done by Bruckner's circle of students. Franz Grasberger comments:

'The four-hand arrangements of his symphonies by students and disciples in the *Wagner-Verein* corresponded neither in principle nor in detail with what he ultimately desired but they represented at least a form of tonal realisation at a time when it was initially very difficult for him to secure orchestral performances and when, later, he still had to struggle to have them played in their proper setting.'[70]

Like those of Bruckner, Mahler's symphonies have been transcribed by a number of different people. His publishers were keen to popularise his music and issued duet arrangements of each work which they made available to libraries and conservatories as well as the public at large. For the most part, Mahler had little to do with their production apart from giving his initial consent and final approval.

Bruno Walter (1876-1962), the conductor and life-long advocate of Mahler, arranged the First Symphony for piano duet. This was published in 1899, alongside the orchestral score. Walter had attended the local première in Weimar of Mahler's First Symphony in June 1894 and became his closest associate at the Vienna State Opera where Mahler was Music Director. The two remained firm friends until the death of Mahler in 1911. Walter wrote:

'As he grew to understand the impassioned interest I felt for his creative work, he began to take pleasure in introducing it to me on the piano, and even today, I still feel the great emotion that the discovery, through him, of his First Symphony kindled in me. Particularly precious in my memory are the occasions when we played piano duets, Schubert being our favourite along with Mozart, Schumann then Wagner and Mahler. As I got to know him better, thanks to our discussions, and to also know the books he read and the philosophers he liked, my initial impression, that of a fantastic and diabolical apparition gave way to a sounder, more complex feeling.'[71]

Aiming to represent the original score as accurately as possible, the opening includes 56 bars of a tremolando 'A' to simulate the mysterious string sound at the beginning of the work. It is interesting to note that the pianist Chitose Okashiro has recently recorded her own piano solo transcription of this symphony, based upon Walter's duet version.[72] She criticises Walter's version as being too literal, not pianistic enough. She attempts, in her own transcription, to recreate the 'essence' of the work rather than simply transcribe as many notes as possible.

Okashiro's performance is certainly impressive – a pianistic 'tour-de-force' no less. However, one might argue that she attempts to make up for the limitations of just one performer by including deliberately 'showy' gestures – huge block chords, over-accentuated dynamics, wayward tempi, utilising extreme high or low registers not used in the original and so on. Her transcription aims to match the impact of the original orchestral work but, in doing so, the ear focuses upon the dazzling technical display rather than the intrinsic musical content. Compared with this, Walter's duet version (as performed by the Prague Piano Duo – see Selected Discography) is an altogether different listening experience. The transcription does not seek to compete with the original, but re-casts the work in a precise, exacting and tempered manner.

Looking carefully through Walter's duet arrangement, one begins to appreciate the clarity of the piano writing. For the most part, Walter's primo and secondo are equally matched, both parts aimed at the good amateur rather than the professional pianist. Throughout the transcription he refers to the original score, often highlighting the difficulties of reproducing the work on the piano. A case in point is the opening of the work (the held 'A') where Walter states (and concedes) that the piano cannot adequately recreate the constant tone of the violins.

Mahler's Second Symphony initially appeared in print in a two piano arrangement by Hermann Behn (1857-1927), a Hamburg lawyer, composer and patron of Mahler who had financed the first orchestral performance of the work. This was published in 1895 by Friedrich Hofmeister in Leipzig. The full score was published two years later. In 1897 Hofmeister was taken over by Josef Weinberger and Bruno Walter was commissioned to produce the transcription of the Second Symphony for piano duet. This is notably more virtuostic than his earlier transcription of the First. Vocal lines are incorporated within the piano texture and text printed (but for reference only). Mahler's Second Symphony needs seven percussion players. Walter solved the problem of recreating the percussion sounds by largely ignoring them – a rather elegant solution to a somewhat impossible situation. An eight-hand version by Heinrich von Bocklet was published by Universal Edition, Vienna, in 1914. Hermann Behn's transcription is particularly interesting in that it contains Mahler's original programmatic indications – later withdrawn by the composer.

The Third Symphony was arranged for piano by the Polish virtuoso pianist Ignaz Friedman (1882-1948). Following the first orchestral performance of the Third, Egon Wellesz (1885-1974), the Austrian composer and musicologist, went to the Vienna Institute of Musicology, where he then was a student and located the piano reduction of the symphony in order to study the work. His duet partner was Anton Webern (1883-1945). The Fourth Symphony was transcribed by the Austrian composer Josef Venantuis von Wöss.

Mahler himself made a piano roll recording using the superior Welte-Mignon system (perfected in Germany in 1903) which could capture not only the notes, but also the dynamics, accents, attacks and pedalling of the pianist, on 9 December 1905 of the fourth movement of this symphony, together with the first movement of the Fifth (transcribed by Otto Singer for piano solo). These actually became the only documents in existence of him as a performer as there are no surviving recordings or films of Mahler as conductor or pianist. After recording he wrote in the Welte studio guestbook 'In my astonishment and admiration, I join with those who preceded me.'[73] Much to the annoyance of Mahler, the rolls failed to sell in any large quantity, mainly due to the fact that they were so expensive at that time. The Fifth Symphony recording cost the equivalent of £115 at today's prices. Despite this, a whole host of other composers began to record for the Welte company and in the following years, the costs reduced substantially, resulting in the pianola (or player-piano) having a brief period of significance in the history of keyboard music. Mahler's Third Symphony later appeared in the Welte catalogue, performed by Hans Haass. The Fifth Symphony was transcribed for piano duet by Otto Singer and was also transcribed for two pianos, four hands by August Stradel (1860-1930), reputed to be one of

Franz Liszt's best pupils. Both editions were published by C. F. Peters.

Alexander von Zemlinsky (1872-1942), co-founder of the 'Alliance of Creative Musicians' alongside Arnold Schoenberg (1874-1951), arranged the Sixth Symphony for piano duet and the transcription appeared in the same year as the orchestral première (1906). Mahler and Zemlinsky are known to have performed the work to Schoenberg at Mahler's house that year and, given this, the transcription might be seen as being 'authentic' (or as near to as might be possible). This work, especially in duet form, became a favourite of Schoenberg. No stranger to transcribing large-scale works, Zemlinsky also arranged Haydn's oratorios *The Seasons* and *The Creation*, Mendelssohn's *St. Paul* Op. 36 and *Elijah* Op. 70 oratorios and Mozart's opera *The Magic Flute* for piano duet.

The order of the movements in the transcription equate with Mahler's original concept of the work (the inner movements being a scherzo followed by the slow movement). It was whilst rehearsing the work, ready for its first performance in Essen (May 1906), that Mahler changed his mind with regard to the order of the inner movements, despite the fact that the scores had already been printed. This 'second thoughts' order has been the subject of some controversy for many years but modern scholarship has clarified the issue. According to Dr. Reinhold Kubik (Editor-in-Chief of the Critical Edition of Mahler's Complete Works) in spite of claims to the contrary, it is now known that Mahler followed the revised order in every single performance of the work he conducted. Consequently, the two recordings of the piano transcription have the scherzo following the andante (see Selected Discography).

The orchestral forces Mahler calls for in this symphony are massive by any standards. Whilst the woodwind instruments are fairly standard, the brass section is notably larger with eight horns, six trumpets, four trombones and tuba. However, it is in the percussion section where there are the more unusual additions. Two sets of timpani, bass drum, triangle, rute (a cylindrical bunch of twigs or cane tied at one end), tam-tam, cowbells, other bells of indeterminate pitch, celesta, xylophone and hammer all appear in the score. The three blows of the latter in the last movement have been the subject of much discussion — were they a premonition of the three blows of fate that fell on Mahler in 1907 — his illness, the death of his daughter and his leaving of Vienna?

Zemlinsky's transcription is a remarkable achievement in that it manages to condense Mahler's often huge score into a readily-playable, non-fussy four staves. Zemlinsky chooses the most important elements of the score and divides these equally amongst the two players. For example, in the final movement, at bar 12 of rehearsal point 133, Mahler's original score has 37 notated parts but Zemlinsky reduces this to just 10 notes, equally distributed between the primo and secondo.

Mahler first conducted his Seventh Symphony in Prague, September 1908. During the rehearsal period, he made numerous revisions and corrections to the score which was eventually published by Bote and Bock. The Italian composer, conductor and pianist, Alfredo Casella (1883-1947), who emerged as one of the most important figures in Italian cultural circles, transcribed the Seventh Symphony for piano duet. Unlike all the other Mahler transcribers, Casella neither lived in Vienna nor knew the composer particularly well. Casella had met Mahler for the first time in Paris in 1909 and subsequently wrote a number of articles about Mahler and his music. Mahler, in turn, persuaded his new publisher, Universal Edition of Vienna, to publish some of Casella's compositions. This was seemingly enough to secure Casella the job of transcribing the Seventh Symphony. Given the almost universal success Mahler was now achieving, being given such a task was highly prestigious.

Casella based his transcription on the now-revised version of the symphony and completed it by the end of 1910. The transcription itself was extremely precise with Casella indicating the instruments Mahler had originally used as well as including additional passages which could not be included in the four-hand texture.

The piano duet transcription of the Eighth Symphony is clouded in mystery with no-one credited as producing the score. Initially, a pianist named Albert Neufelt had been commissioned to produce the arrangement, but this was deemed to be unsatisfactory. Alban Berg (1885-1935) then worked on the score but used the vocal score already prepared by Josef Venantuis von Wöss as a basis for the transcription. The American musicologist Susan M. Miller suggests that the publisher decided not to acknowledge the authorship of the arrangement due to the difficulty of assessing who had actually made it. Berg himself was not unhappy with this situation as he himself came to question the quality of the transcription. Josef Venantuis von Wöss also made the duet version of Mahler's Ninth Symphony which was published in 1912.

Although Mahler never transcribed his own orchestral work, he did take a keen interest in the arrangements that were made by others. As an arranger, he 're-scored' several major works including symphonies by Beethoven and Schumann.

Franck, Saint-Saëns and Debussy

César Franck (1822-1890), Belgian by birth but spending most of his life in France, is perhaps best known as an organist, yet contributed a great deal to the piano repertoire, particularly in his early composing career — one which was characterised by sporadic outbursts of creativity and several fallow periods.

Franck's initial plans to be a composer, fuelled by his father's active encouragement, eventually developed into a desire to become a piano virtuoso. Lack of sustained success in this field finally lead him into teaching and taking a post as organist at the church of Notre-Dame de Lorette. From then he took up a series of organist posts and became associated with the famous organ builder Cavaillé-Coll, whose instruments very much helped to define the French style of organ composition. An influential teacher, his pupils (known as the 'bande à Franck') included Duparc (1848-1933), d'Indy (1851-1931), Ropartz (1864-1955), Dukas (1865-1935), Pierné (1863-1937), Guilmant (1837-1911), Magnard (1865-1914) and Tournemire (1870-1939). Franck's influence as regards form and harmony in particular, thus stretched way into the twentieth century, touching a whole generation of French composers.

It was in the last fifteen years of his life that Franck composed the greater part of his symphonic work including the symphonic poems *Les Éolides* (1876), *Le Chasseur Maudit* (1882), *Les Djinns* (1884) *Psyché* (1887), the *Variations Symphoniques* (1885) and the Symphony in D minor (1888). All of these works were transcribed for four hands by the composer (*Le Chasseur Maudit, Les Djinns* and the Symphony for piano duet and the other works for two pianos).

À mon ami Henri Duparc

SYMPHONIE
pour Orchestre
par
CÉSAR FRANCK

Partition d'Orchestre, net 30 Fr.   *Parties d'Orchestre, net 60 Fr.

Réduction pour Piano à 4 mains par l'auteur, net Fr. 10.—
Réduction pour Piano à 2 mains . . . . net Fr. 7.—
La même pour Violon et Piano . . . . net Fr. 7.—
Symphonie arrangée en trio pour V^{on}, V^{celle} et
    Piano . . . . net Fr. 12.—
Allegretto de la Symphonie, pour Piano seul net Fr. 2.50

Du même auteur:

Sonate P^o et V^{on}, transcrite à 2 mains par A. Cortot net Fr. 6.—
Sonate P^o et V^{on}, transcrite à 4 mains par A. Cortot net Fr. 8.—
Prélude, Aria et Final à 2 mains . . . . net Fr. 4.—
Quatuor à cordes, transcrit à 4 mains . . . . . . net Fr. 10.—
Quintette P^o et cordes, transcrit à 4 mains . . . . net Fr. 10.—
Andante du quatuor à cordes transcrit pour
    Piano et violon . . . . net Fr. 2.50

Propriété pour tous pays
Tous droits d'exécution, d'arrangements et de reproduction réservés

Paris, J. HAMELLE, Editeur
Ancne Mson J. Maho

22, Boulevard Malesherbes, 22

* La copie des parties est interdite et sera légalement poursuivie

This title page shows the number of different arrangements Franck
made of his Symphony.

The fact that Franck transcribed all the orchestral works himself, rather than allow others to do the task, shows clearly how importantly he viewed the act of transcription as an artistic expression rather than just a necessary process. Certainly, his orchestral work became more widely known through these transcriptions, all of which were published before the full scores. In fact, by the time of Franck's death, only *Le Chasseur Maudit* was published in full score, whereas several of the piano transcriptions were available in print.

Franck suffered from a mixed critical reception throughout his career and, despite several attempts, failed to assert himself as a great operatic composer. *Hulda* − an uncompromising work based on the sombre play by the Norwegian playwright Björnson, occupied Franck for a six year period (1879-1885) but was never performed in his lifetime. As a method of publicising the work, he transcribed some of the most important symphonic passages for piano duet (the *Entr'acte pastoral* of the Third Act) and two pianos (the *Chanson de l'Hermine, Marche Royale* and *Ballet du Printemps* which is almost a symphonic suite in itself, being in five movements).

Born just eight years after the death of Beethoven and surviving Debussy by three years, Camille Saint-Saëns embraced a period of rapidly evolving musical change, in a composing career stretching for almost eighty years.

A child prodigy in every sense of the word, Saint-Saëns made his professional debut at the Salle Pleyel, Paris, at the age of ten, playing solo piano pieces and concertos by Mozart and Beethoven. Never easily fitting into the typical French stereotype, he was initially hailed by the critics as 'modernist' and 'revolutionary' but, in some eyes, became 'old-fashioned' and 'reactionary' − a view held by both critics and composers. The founder of the 'Société Nationale de Musique', set up to actively promote new French music in 1871, Saint-Saëns was ousted from his post, fifteen years later in a 'coup' fronted by Vincent d'Indy.

The high regard of many composers can be seen by the fact that Saint-Saëns's chamber and orchestral work was transcribed by many of his contemporaries, including Bizet (1838-1875), Fauré (1845-1924), Dukas, Messager (1853-1929), D'Albert (1864-1932) and Debussy. Saint-Saëns had an almost universal relationship with his publisher, Durand, and the company issued numerous versions of his works. The relatively simple Septet Op. 65 originally written for trumpet, two violins, viola, cello, double bass and piano was arranged for piano duet by Fauré, and the composer himself produced a trio version for violin, cello and piano. He later re-arranged the second and fourth movements for two pianos (published as Minuet and Gavotte Op. 65).

Saint-Saëns wrote a number of symphonic poems – the ubiquitous *Dance Macabre* Op. 40 as well as *Le Rouet d'Omphale* Op. 31, *Phaéthon* Op. 39 and *La Jeunesse d'Hercule* Op. 50. He made four-hand arrangements of all these – either for piano duet or two pianos. At the behest of Durand, Saint-Saëns even made a solo version of Op. 31. Other orchestral and concertante works were also transcribed by the composer and Saint-Saëns continued to write a number of original pieces for both piano duet and two pianos.

Saint-Saëns made four-hand arrangements of two of his symphonies – the First Op. 2 for piano duet and the famous Third Op. 78 for two pianos. The Second Symphony Op. 55 was transcribed for two pianos by Debussy – a composer who found little favour with Saint-Saëns.

He was also active in producing piano arrangements of music by other composers, in solo piano, piano duet and two piano formats. Two of the most interesting, if slightly bizarre, are the two piano versions of Liszt's B minor Piano Sonata and Chopin's Piano Sonata No. 2 in B flat minor. Both these were published by Durand and were more likely to be issued for commercial rather than artistic reasons. However, it is documented that Saint-Saëns performed the Liszt arrangement with Louis Diémer (1843-1919), French composer and pianist, in 1914.

Saint-Saëns was a master of transcription, arranging numerous duets and extending the two piano repertoire.

Tchaikovsky's patron, Nadezhda von Meck, widow of the Russian railway magnate, Karl von Meck, also had a profound influence on Debussy. From 1880 he was employed by the von Meck household, his duties including teaching her children, playing piano in her own personal trio, accompanying family performances and playing duets with Mme von Meck, including Tchaikovsky's Fourth Symphony Op. 36. She wrote to Tchaikovsky expressing her satisfaction with Debussy.

It was in this year that Debussy made piano duet transcriptions of excerpts from Tchaikovsky's ballet *Swan Lake* Op. 20, at the request of Mme von Meck. These were produced chiefly for additional repertoire for her duet playing with Debussy. With the approval of Tchaikovsky, she had these published by Jurgenson in Moscow. However, Debussy's name was not credited as the transcriber. Such a credit may have infuriated his teachers in Paris.

Debussy (third along) with the other two members of the von Meck household trio, pictured in 1880.

Whilst in the employ of the von Meck household, Debussy conceived an orchestral Symphonie consisting of four movements between 1880 and 1882. The first movement was arranged for piano duet in 1880 and presented to Mme von Meck the following year. Discovered in Russia in 1925, it was eventually published in 1933. The remaining movements are either lost or were, perhaps, never actually written down. Sounding more like Brahms or Dvořák than Debussy, the work nevertheless contains flashes of originality that were later to become the trademarks of the Debussy style.

Throughout his career, Debussy appeared in public concerts, as solo pianist, accompanist and as one half of a piano duet, performing works by himself and those of others. At the Grand Prix de Rome, 1884, he played piano duet with René Chansarel, accompanying singers in his cantata *L'Enfant Prodigue* which won first prize. With pianist Jaques Durand he performed his own *Petit Suite* and a duet transcription of Rimsky-Korsakov's *Capriccio Espanol* Op. 34. With Ricardo Vines he performed his own transcriptions of *Nocturnes* and *Iberia*, the latter at a special gala concert at the Comédie des Champs Elysées in June 1913.

Debussy was well-known to other composers as a most accomplished pianist. With the composer and pianist Paul Vidal (1863-1931), he performed a duet arrangement of Liszt's *Faust* Symphony in the presence of the composer in 1886. Apparently, Liszt fell to sleep during the performance.

Debussy's most celebrated orchestral works, *Prelude à l'après midi d'un faune* and *La Mer* were both transcribed for four hands by the composer. The duet version of *La Mer* was completed on 5 March 1905 – several months before the completed orchestral score was sent to the publisher, Durand. Both versions were published at the same time in 1905. André Caplet (1878-1925) made a six-hand arrangement in 1908 (unpublished) and a two piano arrangement in 1909, published by Durand. It is interesting to note that the revisions Debussy made to *La Mer* in 1909 were never incorporated into the duet version.

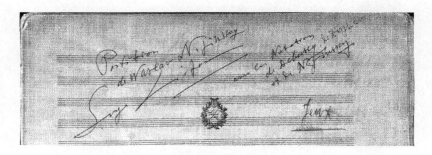

Debussy made a piano reduction of the ballet *Jeux* specifically for Ballets Russes rehearsals before the first performance in May 1913. He used four staves for several sections of the work indicating that ideally two players were needed. This is the title page from the copyists score on which the dancer Serge Lifar has written 'Partition de Waslaw Nijinsky avec les notations de Debussy, de Diaghilev et de Nijinsky'. It was issued in this form by Durand before the printed copy was engraved.

Debussy at the home of Ernest Chausson (1855-1899), playing a
duet with Madame Chausson in 1893. Chausson himself composed
just a couple of piano duets.

The 'symphonic' transcription for piano duet reached its pinnacle
during this century. The next century would see its eventual decline
and fall, largely as a result of emerging new technology developed by
two men – Thomas Edison (1847-1931), inventor of the
phonograph in 1877 and Emile Berliner (1851-1929) inventor of the
gramophone disc from 1887 onwards.

The Twentieth Century

Despite Edison's invention of the phonograph in the latter part of the nineteenth century and Berliner's subsequent development of the gramophone disc allowing the mass reproduction of sound recordings – the first coin operated machines capable of playing back recorded music were installed in America in 1889 – it would be incorrect to assume that this had an immediate impact upon the production of piano duet transcriptions of symphonic music or piano transcriptions as a whole. Early acoustic recordings were of relatively poor quality and focussed mainly on the popular song or 'light' repertoire. It was not until 1913 that a major conductor entered the recording studio – Artur Nikisch conducting Beethoven's Fifth Symphony with the Berlin Philharmonic.

Not until the advent of electrical recording in the mid-1920s did a serious challenge emerge. HMV issued the first electrically recorded symphony recording in 1925, nearly fifty years after sound recording had been made possible. This largely explains the fact that there was no significant decrease in published transcriptions in the first quarter of the century.

There was also a vociferous body of composers, publishers and intellectuals who vehemently opposed this new technology. Their arguments concerning the demise of the live performance were, in many senses, proved right, though not immediately, as was feared.

The English Tradition

English music underwent somewhat of a renaissance in the late nineteenth and early twentieth centuries. Edward Elgar emerged as one of the leading composers of his generation, finding favour on both the home and international stage. Significantly, Elgar was one of the first composers to embrace the new possibilities of recording sound and he made numerous recordings of his own work for HMV – first acoustically and then electronically as the technology developed. This advocacy was highly significant, influencing a new generation of English composers. The importance of these recordings can be seen in the fact that most are still available today, with 'legendary' status.

In 1899, his first major orchestral work, the *Enigma Variations* Op. 36 was premièred in London under the baton of Hans Richter (1888-1976). Previous to this, Elgar had made a solo piano transcription which he sent to the publisher, Novello in March 1898. It was normal practice for Elgar to complete a piano arrangement before going on to score a work for full orchestra.

Though not a formidable pianist – his output for the piano was relatively small – Elgar enjoyed occasions when he could play duets with his friends at various social gatherings. Jerrold Northrop Moore refers to an evening when Elgar was entertaining friends and sight-reading Tchaikovsky's duet transcription of his Sixth Symphony:

'Musicians were all agog about the 5/4 movement. Elgar tackled the bass part but he soon got into a mess and had to stop. After another attempt he eventually reached the end and remarked 'The violin is my instrument – not the piano!' [74]

When discussing the music of Frederick Delius, the contribution of his amanuensis, Eric Fenby (1906-1997), is widely recognised. Less well-known is the relationship between Delius and Philip Heseltine – better known as the composer, Peter Warlock.

Heseltine became interested in the music of Delius while a scholar at Eton College and got to know Delius personally through an uncle who lived close to the composer's French home. Their friendship and collaboration lasted until Heseltine's early death in 1930. Their correspondence numbers well over four hundred letters.

Delius at the piano.

Heseltine aka Warlock.

As a composer of primarily small-scale chamber works, including many songs with piano accompaniment, Heseltine was a master at the keyboard, possessing the many skills required to produce successful transcriptions. Like a number of other composers at this time, he was greatly interested by the possibilities of the player piano (or pianola) and spent many hours listening to classical works on this medium. He made his enthusiasm clear to Delius who was equally keen to see some of his music transcribed for the player piano. Unfortunately, his publisher, Augener, was less keen and only the *Entracte* from his opera *A Village Romeo and Juliet* appeared in the pianola catalogue. Delius was extremely frustrated at this situation as he firmly believed that the pianola could serve a very useful role in allowing the public to familiarise themselves with the great orchestral works – including his own.

113

Heseltine's first Delius arrangement was of *Brigg Fair* in 1911 for two pianos. Subsequently he produced piano duet versions of several orchestral works including: *In a Summer Garden*, *On Hearing the First Cuckoo in Spring*, *Summer Night on the River*, *North Country Sketches*, *A Song Before Sunrise* and the two *Dance Rhapsodies*. In most cases, the transcriptions were produced either two or three years after the original orchestral versions. However, there was a seven year gap before Heseltine produced a duet transcription of the *North Country Sketches*. Robert Threlfall recounts that:

'On publication, Heseltine's arrangement was hailed as 'the perfection of editing' by a reviewer who had 'never seen any work of this kind more thoroughly and sensibly done.' This particularly pleased Heseltine because it supported 'the view which ....you [FD] hold also, that a piano transcription is first and foremost a guide to the orchestral score and only quite secondarily a piano piece (unless it is simply a pianist's free fantasia, and this only a Liszt or Busoni can do.....to another composer's work).' [75]

Living in France, Delius associated himself with a number of leading French composers. Florent Schmitt (1870-1958) transcribed several excerpts from the opera *Irmelin*. Ravel (1875-1937) was commissioned to produce a piano reduction and vocal edition of Delius' one-act opera *Margot la Rouge*. However, in correspondence between Ravel and Delius, Ravel asked:

'Please let me know if it is absolutely necessary to transcribe the prelude for two hands. A four-hand transcription would be considerably more effective.' [76]

As the transcription appeared for piano solo only, one assumes that either Delius or, more likely, his publisher refused this request.

Following on from Elgar and Delius, we see the decline in popularity of the piano transcription in English music. When considering the music of Holst (1874-1934), Ireland (1879-1962), Bridge (1879-1941), Bax (1883-1953), Walton (1902-1983), Tippett (1905-1998), Britten and Arnold, there are just a few notable examples.

Holst made both two piano and duet reductions of *The Planets* Op. 32. Published in 1949, the original manuscripts of the two piano version are divided between the Royal College of Music, the Royal Academy of Music and the British Library. The duet version was recently discovered at St. Paul's Girls' School, Hammersmith, by piano tutor John York. It had been made under Holst's supervision by fellow staff members of the school – Vally Lasker and Nora Day and autographed by the composer. Sir Adrian Boult, who conducted the first performance of the work in 1918, recalled hearing Lasker and Day performing the duet transcription a year earlier. Tim Munday's two piano, eight-hand transcription, was first performed at Firth Hall, Sheffield in 1986.[77]

Britten made a two piano arrangement of his *Paul Bunyon* Overture (following the withdrawal of the full version of the work after unfavourable reviews in 1941) and Constant Lambert (1905-1951) made several duet transcriptions of music by Walton (the *Façade Suites*) and Vaughan Williams (*The Wasps: Aristophanic Suite*).

Music in Vienna

In 1918, Schoenberg was instrumental in the setting up the 'Society for Private Musical Performances' along with Webern, Berg and the Polish pianist Eduard Steuermann (1892-1964). The Society had three main aims, outlined in a policy document written by Berg:

1. Performances should be clear and well-rehearsed.
2. There should be frequent repetitions and performances given privately, away from 'the corrupting influence of publicity'.
3. All types of music were to be encouraged – only the worthless being excluded.

The setting up of the Society was very much a reaction to the ending of the war and the need to re-establish the musical and other cultural frameworks of central Europe and Austria in particular.

For a period of three years, over one hundred concerts were given, featuring the music of well-over one hundred and fifty contemporary works. In the first season alone, twenty-six concerts featuring the music of forty-five composers were presented. Significantly, orchestral works were usually performed in piano transcriptions for either four or eight hands by the original composer or specially chosen arranger. This was largely due to financial considerations and for ease of programming. The very first concert was devoted to Casella's duet transcription of Mahler's Seventh Symphony, performed by Steuermann and Ernst Bachrich (1892-1942).

In the bylaws of the Society, the following passage referred to the importance of adequate rehearsal:

'The works are to be prepared for performance with a meticulousness and thoroughness lacking in today's concert practice. If in today's concert practice one generally has to get along as best as one can with an arbitrarily set and always insufficient number of rehearsals, then the criteria for determining the number of rehearsals in the society shall be the achievement of the greatest possible clarity and the fulfilment of the composer's complete intention insofar as it is reflected in the work. A work cannot and shall not be presented in the society until these basic preconditions for a good performance, namely clarity and precision, have been met.'[78]

Schoenberg coached Steuermann and Bachrich in no less than thirty separate rehearsals in preparation for the performance, reflecting his own love of the music and his determination to make this new musical venture a success.

The following selection of orchestral works programmed by the 'Verein für musikalische Privataufführungen' 1918-1921 certainly satisfies Berg's third aim:

Franz Schmidt (1874-1939):
Symphony No.2 arr. piano duet by Alexander Wunderer.
Franz Schreker (1878-1934):
Prelude to a Drama arr. piano duet by the composer.
Gustav Mahler:
Symphony No.6 arr. piano duet by Zemlinksy.
Symphony No.7 arr. piano duet by Alfred Casella.
Richard Strauss:
Don Quixote arr. piano duet by Otto Singer.
Sinfonia Domestica arr. two pianos by Otto Singer.
Claude Debussy:
Three Nocturnes arr. piano duet by Ravel.
Anton Webern:
Passacaglia arr. two pianos, six hands.
Arnold Schoenberg – *Pelleas and Melisande* arr. piano duet by Heinrich Jalowetz (1882-1946), a student of Schoenberg and 'core' member of the Second Viennese School.
Béla Bartók:

117

Rhapsody for Piano and Orchestra arr. two pianos by the composer.
Igor Stravinsky:
Petrushka arr. piano duet by the composer.

Schoenberg himself made duet transcriptions of his two Chamber Symphonies Op. 9 and 38, Berg also transcribed the First Chamber Symphony and arranged *Gurrelieder* for four hands and Webern made a two piano arrangement of Schoenberg's Five Pieces for Orchestra Op. 16.

Schoenberg transcribed Rossini's opera *The Barber of Seville* for piano duet in 1903. His Six Pieces for Piano Four Hands (1895-96) are, surprisingly, no more extreme.

Another composer famed for his arrangements was Max Reger (1873-1916). Reger's duet transcriptions of the works of J. S. Bach, including the Brandenburg Concertos, Orchestral Suites and numerous organ pieces have remained popular up to this day. However, his reductions of several Wagner overtures went out of print almost as soon as they were published.

The Russian Tradition

In Russia, the well-established practice of transcribing orchestral works for piano continued well into the twentieth century. The next generation of composers following 'The Mighty Handful', including Glazunov, Scriabin and Rachmaninov all made significant contributions to the medium.

Of these three, Glazunov's transcriptions for piano duet are the most numerous. As well as many smaller orchestral compositions, Glazunov arranged four of his symphonies for duet – Nos. 2, 3, 4 and 7. Mme. Rimsky-Korsakova (Nadezhda Purgold) transcribed the First Symphony and Rachmaninov transcribed the Sixth. Glazunov's final completed symphony – the Eighth – was first heard in a four-hand arrangement performed at the home of Rimsky-Korsakov, January 1906. Glazunov also made eight-hand arrangements of his orchestral fantasies *The Forest* Op. 19 and *The Sea* Op. 28.

The Sixth Symphony was premièred alongside the first performance of Rachmaninov's First Symphony with Glazunov conducting the orchestra. The disastrous failure of the latter has been blamed on the poor conducting of Glazunov. He was notoriously weak in this area – though it is generally accepted that there was little rehearsal time and Glazunov, fearing the worst, consoled himself with alcohol. Rachmaninov's First was never again performed in the composer's lifetime and, following the critical mauling he received, the composer sank into a deep depression which robbed him of three years musical creativity. The original parts of the work were thought lost but the complete score was reconstructed after the parts were eventually discovered, with the duet transcription used as a guide.

Rachmaninov also produced four-hand versions of his Second and Fourth Piano Concertos and his Symphonic Dances Op. 45. A master of the solo piano transcription, Rachmaninov's four-hand arrangements are no-less expert.

Scriabin found enthusiastic support from Belyayev, despite his increasingly strange theosophic beliefs. Beginning essentially as a piano miniaturist, Scriabin became obsessed by producing orchestral music of massive grandeur, synthesising all the arts.

All of Scriabin's major orchestral works have been transcribed for either piano duet or two pianos. Alexander Winkler (1865-1935), who taught at the St. Petersburg Conservatory and worked for the publisher, Belyayev, transcribed the First Symphony Op. 26 (1899-1900). The Second Symphony Op. 29 (1901) was transcribed by the Russian composer and academic Vasily (Basil) Kalafati (1869-1942). The Third Symphony *The Divine Poem* Op. 43 (1902-04) was transcribed by Lev Konyus, who also transcribed the *Poem of Ecstasy* Op. 54 (1905-08). Scriabin used the four-hand version of the Third Symphony to promote its recognition, performing it to several European conductors. Scriabin himself had been asked to produce the piano version of this work but failed to complete the task. How much of the published arrangement is in fact by Scriabin rather than Konyus is undocumented. One might expect the piano transcription to be a pale imitation of the original, but, in fact, it retains the grandeur of Scriabin's vision and improves upon the clarity of the orchestral lines. Only the opulence of the scoring is lost. Leonid Sabaneyev (1881-1968), friend and follower of Scriabin, transcribed his final completed work of 1910 *Prometheus: Poem of Fire* Op. 60. Scriabin believed that eight hands were necessary for any arrangement of this latter work and expressed discontent when he learnt that Sabaneyev had completed the task without needing to double the forces required to perform the music.

With the Revolution and subsequent creation of the Soviet Union the practice of transcription became particularly important, as orchestral performances were subject to political intervention with state control of concert halls. It was far easier to suppress a full orchestral performance of a work than a transcription that could be performed in virtually any location, at any time and by just two performers.

The playing of piano duets played an important part in the musical education and development of Prokofiev (1891-1953). As a student he played a four-hand piano transcription of his own (unpublished) Symphony in G with Taneyev at the St. Petersburg Conservatory. One of his earliest works was a transcription of themes from Rimsky-Korsakov's *Scheherazade* Op. 35. In his memoirs, he recounts:

'the visit in December 1906 of Reger, who conducted his Serenade in G major, made a deep impression on me. Myaskovsky surprised me one day by producing from his portfolio a four-hand arrangement of the Serenade. We sat down and played it then and there. Shortly after that Myaskovsky came to my house to play Beethoven's Ninth Symphony with me. He said no one had ever been able to play it with him to the end.'[79]

Myaskovsky (1881-1950) remained a friend for the rest of his life and the two composers often played duets together, comparing work. Myaskovsky, composer of twenty-seven symphonies, arranged many of his own works for piano duet. Prokofiev made his own four-hand piano transcriptions of his First Symphony Op.25, the ballet *Romeo and Juliet* Op. 64, the opera *The Love for Three Oranges* Op. 33 and he also sanctioned arrangements made by others. For example, the English composer, Thomas Dunhill (1877-1946) made an 'easy' piano version of *Peter and the Wolf* Op. 67. This was a huge success and did much to popularise Prokofiev's music in England. Unusually, it remains in print today. Anatoly Ivanovich Vedernikov (b. 1920) – Soviet pianist and graduate of the Moscow Conservatory, made four-hand arrangements of Prokofiev's Seventh Symphony Op. 131 and several other pieces of orchestral music. Just before his death, Prokofiev asked Vedernikov to make a piano score of the ballet *The Tale of the Stone Flower* Op. 118.

121

Like Prokofiev, Stravinsky spent time playing duets with fellow students and teachers as a method of learning music both old and new. He would often visit the apartment of Rimsky-Korsakov, his composition tutor at the St. Petersburg Conservatory and play piano duets.

Following its successful première at the Paris Opera in June 1910, Stravinsky's first major success, the ballet *The Firebird*, was published for solo piano in the same year (arranged by the composer). Stravinsky had already played a reduction for the Ballets Russes rehearsals and such an arrangement was seen as a way to popularise the music.

Stravinsky composed almost exclusively at the piano. He felt it necessary to be able to physically hear and feel the harmony and texture of the sound he was creating. With his pianist son, Soulima, he often played duets and, not surprisingly, arranged some of his ballets for this medium. He commented:

'All my life I have tried out my music as I have composed it, orchestral as well as any other kind, four hands at one keyboard... the instrument itself is the center of my life and the fulcrum of all my musical discoveries. Each note that I write is tried on it, and every relationship of notes is taken apart and heard on it again and again. '[80]

Peter Hill elaborates on this matter:

'Stravinsky saw the piano as a source of the unexpected, enabling him to seize on the possibilities glimpsed, perhaps, in the mere slip of a finger. Originating as they did in this way, it is no surprise that many of Stravinsky's orchestral works translate marvellously well back into the medium of the piano; even specifically orchestral effects – the hammered string chords which open the *Dances of the Young Girls* in *The Rite of Spring* turn out to 'fit' perfectly as they explode under the pianist's hands. Moreover, by exercising our historical imagination, the arrangement for piano of *The Rite of Spring* gives us a sense of a masterpiece at an early stage of its discovery.'[81]

Stravinsky made his transcription of *The Rite of Spring* before the orchestration was completed and it was used at ballet rehearsals. A pianistic 'tour de force', the players interweave fingers, hands and sometimes arms, in order to meet Stravinsky's tremendous technical demands for virtuosity. Almost a year before its notorious first performance in Paris, Stravinsky had played the duet version with Debussy. Following this, Debussy wrote to Stravinsky:

'Our reading at the piano of *Le Sacre du Printemps* is always in my mind. It haunts me like a beautiful dream, and I will try in vain to reinvoke the terrific impression. That is why I wait for the stage performance like a greedy child impatient for sweets.'[82]

Pierre Monteux (1875-1964), the French conductor, was visited by Stravinsky before he conducted the orchestral première of the work. Monteux recalled:

'Stravinsky sat down to play a piano reduction of the entire score. Before he got very far I was convinced he was raving mad. Heard in this way, without the color of the orchestra, which is one of its greatest distinctions, the crudity of the rhythm was emphasised, its dark primitiveness underlined. The very walls resounded as Stravinsky pounded away, occasionally stamping his feet and jumping up and down, to accentuate the force of the music.'[83]

In this barest of states, the music does seem to be more angular, earthy and bristling with raw energy. The biting dissonance and jagged time-signature shifts are starkly illuminated in the piano transcription. Stephen Walsh, the acclaimed Stravinsky scholar notes that in *The Rite of Spring*, Stravinsky's orchestral layering retains very much the character of the original piano texture and chord layout.[84] Published in 1913, eight years before the orchestral score, the transcription initially did much to popularise the work, as orchestral performances were limited by the impact of the First World War. Later, a solo piano transcription was made by Vladimir Leyetchkiss, Professor of piano, with the full approval of Stravinsky.

Stravinsky also arranged smaller-scale pieces for piano duet. For example, the Three Pieces for String Quartet were composed in 1914 and a duet transcription was made in the same year. The outbreak of war meant that the original string version remained unpublished until 1922 – Stravinsky revising it four years previously. The piano version (not published until 1994) is particularly interesting as it reflects Stravinsky's original thinking, with differences in articulation, pitch and some rhythms. For example, at the beginning of the second movement, the Quartet features repeated triplets, whilst in the piano arrangement, straight quavers are written marked *forte pesante* (the Quartet is marked *piano* with a crescendo to *sforzando*). The revision of the Quartet shows clearly that Stravinsky was aiming to make the music more idiomatic for the strings.

Like Mahler, Stravinsky admired the player-piano and found it to be an ideal medium for transcribing his orchestral works – not tied down by the limits of ten or even twenty digits. During the 1920s, the Paris firm of Pleyel gifted Stravinsky a studio at their Headquarters and, in close cooperation with Jacques Larmanjat, Pleyel's head of music rolls, Stravinsky made new arrangements of *The Firebird, Petrushka, The Rite of Spring, Song of the Nightingale, Pulcinella, Les Noces* and several smaller works. He even composed an Etude pour Pianola, published in 1921. In 1924 Stravinsky began a new contract with the Aeolian Company in New York. In January 1925 he travelled to America for a concert tour and to record some piano rolls for the Duo-Art system. The Sonata for Piano was actually published as a roll before the sheet music was issued.

An advertisement for the Pleyela which appeared in 1921.[85]

Shostakovich (1906-1975) was another Russian composer who was drawn to the piano duet medium. His struggles with the Soviet authorities are well documented and, together with periods of self-doubt in the validity of some of his work, several orchestral works were either withdrawn or lapsed into obscurity. Even today, a significant number of his works remain unpublished.

For example, until its dramatic revival in Moscow in December 1961, Shostakovich's Fourth Symphony Op. 43 was perhaps only known to a relatively small and select group of Soviet musicians. Only a handful of these had heard the work's orchestral debut twenty-five years earlier in 1936. Failing to impress and with Shostakovich reeling from a damning indictment of his opera *Lady Macbeth of Mtsensk* Op. 29 in Pravda ('Muddle instead of Music' rumoured to be written by

Stalin himself), the work was withdrawn at the request of the Composers' Union leadership. Fearing a political backlash, Shostakovich readily agreed to this, famously referring to his Fifth Symphony Op. 47 as 'a Soviet Artist's reply to just criticism'. The Fourth Symphony only survived in a piano duet version made by the composer in 1936 (published in 1946 in a limited print-run of three hundred copies and again in 2000 as part of the New Shostakovich Edition).

This was performed by the composer and Moisei Vainberg (1919-1996) at a closed meeting of the Composers' Union just after the ending of the Second World War. In 1948 the piano reduction was officially banned and withdrawn from circulation.

Shostakovich's arrangement is a straight-forward transcription of the original work and reveals, in great clarity, Shostakovich as a master of contrapuntal technique – he was, after all, a great admirer of Bach. In the orchestral version, the sheer weight of orchestral sound that is employed can cloud this impression. The percussive nature of the piano also adds to the overall realisation that this is a highly charged work, full of nervous energy.

The young composer Boris Tischenko (b. 1939) decided to perform the work with Professor Dmitriev of the Leningrad Conservatory in the presence of the composer, as part of the institution's centenary celebrations in 1960. This encouraged Shostakovich's assistant, Lev Atovmyan, to track down the original orchestral parts, missing since the Second World War, from which the score could then be re-assembled. This was then finally given official Soviet approval.

In the DSCH Journal, Pauline Fairclough states:

'As the Fourth Symphony became a well-established feature of orchestral programmes, Shostakovich's old duet version promptly fell into obscurity. It was only ever intended for the practical purpose of disseminating a work that was costly and difficult to perform in an age where large-scale orchestral works were routinely learned through the medium of piano reduction. Long after his younger colleagues had abandoned the practice of teaching repertoire this way in favour of using the gramophone, Shostakovich continued to insist that his students make piano reductions of scores and perform them in class. He clearly believed that such a 'hands-on' approach had a unique value that could not be replicated by listening to records. And it is true that playing orchestral music on the piano can be revelatory, especially in the case of mainstream 'tonal' twentieth century composers like Shostakovich. What sounds deceptively 'normal' played by an orchestra sounds very different on the piano. Stripped of the familiar cloak of instrumental sounds, the off-colour sharpness typical of his skewed diatonicism is often disconcertingly accentuated. In fact, this is so true of the Fourth Symphony's piano duet reduction that it is possible to understand the negative reactions of Shostakovich's contemporaries who had never heard the work in its full orchestral version. The menacing tread of the first movement becomes dryly percussive, while the haunting Mahlerian landler character of the second movement is lost altogether. It isn't hard to imagine a Composers' Union audience totally at sea in the finale, which can be baffling enough at first hearing even in a fine orchestral performance.' [86]

Shostakovich giving a piano recital in 1951.

Sofia Moshevich relates that Shostakovich made a four-hand piano transcription of his Tenth Symphony Op. 93 which he performed with Vainberg at the Moscow Conservatory on 27 October 1953 and

127

soon afterwards in Leningrad for Yevgeniy Mravinsky (1903-1988) and several Leningrad composers. [87] The orchestral première took place on 17 December 1953 under Mravinsky at the Great Philharmonic Hall in Leningrad. On 15 February 1954 they recorded this arrangement (last issue: Revelation Records RV70002). He also performed a four-hand arrangement of his Eleventh Symphony Op. 103 with composer Mikhail Meyerovich (1920-1993) at official gatherings in Leningrad (16 September) and Moscow (25 September).

In fact, Shostakovich transcribed a substantial number of his symphonies, concertos, ballets and film music in one form or another. The following lists his symphony transcriptions for one or two pianos:

Symphony No. 3 in E flat major transcribed for solo piano Op. 20B
Symphony No. 4 in C minor transcribed for piano duet Op. 43B
Symphony No. 9 in E flat major transcribed for piano duet Op. 70B
Symphony No. 10 in E minor transcribed for piano duet Op. 93B
Symphony No. 11 in G minor transcribed for piano duet Op. 103B
Symphony No. 12 in D minor transcribed for piano duet Op. 112B
Symphony No. 13 in B flat major transcribed for two pianos Op. 112B
Symphony No. 15 in A major transcribed for two pianos Op. 141B

Recently Shostakovich's transcriptions have gained somewhat in popularity – seen as important musical documents in their own right. Colin Stone and Rustem Hayroudinoff recorded the Fourth Symphony in 2004 – the first modern recording of a transcription for several decades. Colin Stone, Professor at the Royal Academy of Music, relates that he had no idea that the transcription existed until he was introduced to it by pianist and Shostakovich scholar Raymond Clarke who, in turn, was told of the work by Shostakovich's third wife, Irina. The Ninth Symphony Op. 70 was performed by Vicky

Yannoula and Jakob Fichert at the Queen Elizabeth Hall, London in September 2006, as part of the Shostakovich centenary celebrations.

As well as his own work, Shostakovich made numerous four-hand transcriptions of newly published compositions sent to him by musicologist and editor Pavel Lamm (1882-1951). Amongst these arrangements were works such as Mahler's Ninth Symphony, and Stravinsky's *Symphony of Psalms*. Shostakovich would usually play the lower part while one of his students played the upper. All the other students sat around the piano and followed the score carefully. A rare example, recently published by the French publisher Salabert, is a two piano transcription that Shostakovich made of the Third Symphony *Symphonie Liturgique* by Honegger (1892-1955), written just after the Second World War.

In the 1920s and 30s the 'Lamm Circle' became an important forum for composers and musicians in Moscow. Meeting at Pavel Lamm's apartment, numerous four-hand and eight-hand transcriptions of both Western and Russian music were played, including the entire symphonic canon of Myaskovsky transcribed by either Lamm or the composer himself. Thus a new generation of Soviet composers such as Alexander Gedike (1877-1957), Alexander Alexandrov (1883-1946), Samuel Feinberg (1890-1962) and Vissarion Shebalin (1902-1963) came to appreciate the importance of the piano transcription and the efficacy of the piano duet in particular.

Music in France

Although both Debussy and Saint-Saëns continued composing well into the twentieth century, a new generation of composers emerged at the forefront of French musical life, including Dukas, Roussel (1869-1937), Honegger, Milhaud (1892-1974), Poulenc and, of course, Ravel. All of these composers, to either a greater or lesser extent, kept the practice of piano duet transcription alive.

Of primary importance is Ravel whose first transcriptions were of the music of Debussy - *Prelude à l'après midi d'un faune* for piano duet (Debussy's own transcription was for two pianos) and *Nocturnes*. Like Saint-Saëns, Ravel enjoyed a fruitful partnership with the publishing firm, Durand. In particular, Ravel established close working relationships with Durand's chief proof-reader, Lucien Garban (1877-1959) and editor Leon Roques (1851-1931). Both these men were to transcribe a number of Ravel's orchestral works for piano duet and two pianos. Garban arranged *La Valse, Le Tombeau de Couperin* and the *Valses nobles et sentimentales*. He also produced transcriptions under the pseudonym Roger Branga. Roques produced an acclaimed version of the ballet *Daphnis et Chloe*. Additionally, both also produced transcriptions of other contemporary French music.

Ravel himself transcribed a considerable amount of his own work, including *La Valse*, the String Quartet in F and *Boléro*. Maurice Hinson states that:

'He lavished a great deal of care on these transcriptions and tried to make them as playable as possible. His synthesizing genius produced a uniquely personal style that exploits the use of modal melodies and the intervals of the seventh and ninth. Ravel extended the pianistic traditions of Franz Liszt but expressed himself in a quintessentially French way.'[88]

Similarly, Ravel transcribed a number of his original piano duets for orchestra, such as *Ma Mère l'Oye* and the 1895 *Habanera* for two pianos which became part of the orchestral *Rapsodie espagnole* of 1907.

Of particular note is Ravel's transcription of *Boléro*, composed in 1928, famously described by the composer as 'seventeen minutes of orchestra without any music.' Commissioned by the dancer Ida Rubinstein, it was conceived as a ballet and first performed as such at the Paris Opéra. Ravel gave the music a deliberately Spanish character but also commented:

'I love going over factories and seeing vast machines at work. It is awe-inspiring and great. It was a factory which inspired my *Bolero*. I would like it always to be played with a vast factory in the background.'[89]

Ravel was not alone in his interest of the mechanical. The late 1920s to mid 1930s gave rise to a number of works celebrating this 'new industrial age'. Prokofiev's Second Symphony has a 'mechanical' aspect to it and his ballet *Le Pas d'Acier* Op. 41, celebrating ordinary Soviet life is set in a factory. George Antheil's *Ballet Mécanique* – surely one of the oddest creations in twentieth century music with its combined forces of sixteen player-pianos, electric bells, alarm clock, siren and aircraft propellers – celebrates the emergence of a mechanized age with its relentless rhythms and industrially-charged dynamics.

Seen by many as simply an exercise in orchestration, *Bolero*'s translation to the medium of the piano might appear decidedly odd in the first instance. However, as Gerald Larner suggests:

'The genius of the work is not so much its scoring – which is unfailingly entertaining in its variety and uniquely masterful in its graduated accumulation of colour – as in the judgement of the precise moment when the conflict can no longer go on as the long-term crescendo reaches its height and the orchestration its maximum aggregation, the friction between melody and mechanism finally causes ignition, the tonality lifts off from C major to E major and, as it falls back, the edifice collapses.'[90]

In fact, Ravel made transcriptions for both piano duet and for two pianos in 1929 and 1930 respectively. Ravel's original manuscript of the duet version can be found in the British Library. Whilst there is little doubt that this was done, in part, for commercial gain – the work was a huge success and catapulted Ravel onto the world stage – it would be wrong to suggest that the transcriptions lack artistic merit and should be dismissed, as a number of critics have done. It is interesting to compare the orchestral original with that of the transcriptions – in this case the duet arrangement:

The all-important side drum rhythm is played (on the note 'G') by the secondo. The melody is played by the primo. At Fig. 1 a second flute is added in the orchestral score but there is no difference to the piano transcription. At Fig. 2 the harp part is incorporated into the primo part (second and third beats) and at bar 53 the side drum part moves to the primo for four bars to accommodate the melody (on bassoon) playing in a lower register (secondo). At Fig. 4 Ravel makes no attempt to 'recreate' the pizzicato strings.

The first significant change to the secondo part occurs at Fig. 5, now including the upper string parts as well as the lower ones. The melody is played in octaves (flute and trumpet in the orchestral score). At Fig. 6 the secondo part reverts to the original pattern as the primo plays the saxophone solo (right hand) and upper strings (left hand). This continues into Fig. 7 with the left hand part becoming fuller.

At Fig. 8 the secondo plays as in Fig. 5 allowing the primo to imitate the combination of flute, piccolo and celeste. If anything, the piano transcription emphasises Ravel's 'exotic' tritonal writing at this point, being more pronounced when heard with a single timbre. The right hand is marked *pp* whilst the left – playing the melody in the original key – is marked *mf.* At Fig. 9 the secondo part continues very much as before whilst the primo part plays the now bitonal woodwind parts – the impact of which, again, comes across more markedly than in the orchestral version. Although by this point the orchestral texture has increased significantly, Ravel is careful not to overburden the pianists but does maintain a sense of augmentation.

At Fig. 10 – where we have the trombone solo – Ravel simply repeats Fig. 6 with its saxophone solo. At Fig. 11 the piano texture begins to build up but Ravel's arrangement is still eminently playable. At bar 216 the secondo part picks up the descending melody with the primo, once again, playing the repeated rhythm. There is no significant change from Fig. 12 to 15.

At Fig. 16 the secondo part becomes its fullest in texture. In the primo, the left hand doubles the right hand an octave lower, giving the fullest texture possible (Ravel is now scoring for thirty-six instruments/parts in the orchestra). This texture is maintained until the end of the piece. At Fig. 18 (bars 335-338) Ravel makes one of the few attempts to imitate an orchestral effect (the trombone glissandi) in the secondo part.

As in the orchestral score, the piano arrangement contains little dynamic direction and a successful performance depends entirely upon the skills and interpretive élan of the performers. Any doubters as to the validity of the transcription should listen to the stunning recordings made by Anthony Goldstone and Caroline Clemmow (piano duet version) and Louis Lortie and Hélène Mercier (two piano version).

In many respects, Ravel's piano transcriptions of *Bolero* (the two piano version varies only from the duet in the positioning of notes between the two players) are a triumph. They are successful for a very simple reason - Ravel does not simply attempt to transcribe every orchestral note but 'remoulds' the work to fit its new context. By comparison, Roger Branga's solo transcription (published in the same year as the duet) is pedestrian, over-fussy and truncated (the player is asked to repeat a seventy-four bar passage four times).

Maurice Ravel – one of the very few composers whose compositions have equal regard in both their piano and orchestral guises.

Honegger transcribed several of his symphonic works for piano duet, including *Chant de Joie*, *Pacific 231* and *Pastorale d'Été*. Milhaud, born in the same year as Honegger, also arranged many of his works for either piano duet or two pianos, including *Le Boeuf sur le Toit* Op. 58, *La Création du Monde* Op. 81 and *Scaramouche* Op. 165. These were transcribed for four hands, following the popularity of the original orchestral versions.

Music in America

As American music began to establish itself in the latter half of the nineteenth century, piano duet performances of orchestral works were programmed relatively frequently in several States to satisfy the growing cultural demands of the emerging middle classes. A number of European virtuoso pianists travelled across the Atlantic to give concert tours, playing, almost exclusively, music from Europe. These included Leopold de Meyer (1816-1883), Henri Herz, Sigismund Thalberg (1812-1871), Anton Rubinstein and Hans von Bülow (1830-1894).

Between October 1875 and May 1876, von Bülow travelled across America giving over one hundred recitals. His programmes contained a vast array of transcriptions, arrangements and paraphrases. During the tour he also gave the world première performance of Tchaikovsky's First Piano Concerto in Boston on October 25 – the first Russian performance actually took place a week later. Thalberg, rival of Liszt (the two competed in a famous concert 'duel' in Paris in 1837 – Liszt often cited as the winner), composed many fantasies (or 'Grand fantasies' as he preferred to call them) based on themes from popular operas.

Both Louis Moreau Gottschalk (1829-1869) and Edward MacDowell (1860-1908) did much to establish the American tradition, though both travelled to Europe to study at the Paris Conservatoire before returning to America.

Gottschalk, frequently referred to as the 'American Liszt', arranged many of his pieces for piano duet – expanding solo works and reducing often gigantic orchestral showpieces for the more convenient medium. He transcribed a number of famous works for piano duet including Rossini's *William Tell* Overture which remains in print today. MacDowell, considered by many to be America's first professional composer, transcribed a number of his orchestral poems for piano duet, including *Hamlet-Ophelia* Op. 22, *Lancelot and Elaine* Op. 25 and *Larnia* Op. 29. All these were published by Schirmer of New York – one of the first American music publishers to be established and later to become one of its most important and influential.

Of the prominent twentieth century composers, including Charles Ives (1874-1954), George Gershwin (1898-1937), Roy Harris (1898-1979), Aaron Copland (1900-1990), Elliott Carter (b. 1908), Samuel Barber (1910-1981) and John Cage (1912-1992), only Gershwin and Copland produced a significant number of four-hand piano arrangements of their orchestral work.

In fact, Gershwin's *An American in Paris*, *Rhapsody in Blue*, *Variations on I Got Rhythm* and the Concerto in F for two pianos and *Cuban Overture* for piano duet all began life in this form. Gershwin generally produced a piano score before he began orchestrating a work and these original manuscripts often included indications as to possible scoring. Ferde Grofé used the second piano part of the *Rhapsody* as the basis for his orchestral arrangement – the first part being the piano solo.

Although made in 1928, the arrangement of *An American in Paris* was not premièred until 1984, with Katia and Marielle Labeque performing the work in New York, following the donation of the original manuscript to the American Library of Congress by Ira Gershwin's widow, Leonore. Of some significance, the piano arrangement contains several additional sections (marked by brackets in the score) which do not appear in the orchestrated version. Between the years 1944-1951, Percy Grainger made several arrangements of Gershwin's work, the most celebrated being the two piano *Fantasy on Porgy and Bess*. This was first performed in New York in 1951. Copland arranged *Billy the Kid* and *Cuban Dance* for the same forces.

Leonard Bernstein (1918-1990) transcribed Copland's *El Salon Mexico* for piano duet.

Gershwin at the piano. He met Ravel in New York in 1928. Both men were keen to learn from each other and this can undoubtedly be heard in their subsequent compositions.

Past, Present and Future

Whilst accepting that the importance and, to some extent, the relevance of the piano duet transcription dwindled as the twentieth century progressed, it is certainly without question that in the previous century it had a fundamentally important role – one which has been largely overlooked and undervalued by music historians.

As has been shown, a great many composers either produced their own transcriptions or allowed others to do so, on their behalf. These arrangers were either other composers, students, friends or professional 'house' arrangers employed by a growing number of publishers across Europe. This book has covered a number of important composers and arrangers but has merely 'scratched the surface' – the practice of making transcriptions became so hugely widespread that one can, with some perseverance, discover four-hand arrangements of symphonic works by almost any popular composer of the nineteenth and early twentieth centuries. However, there is an important distinction to be made between those transcriptions made around the time when the original symphonic work was composed and those produced many years later, usually for commercial purposes. The latter are, for the most part, of less intrinsic value.

The huge increase in music publishing that began in the late eighteenth century satisfied a demand from an ever-increasing European (and later American) middle class for four-hand repertoire. This, in turn, was driven by the surge in popularity of the piano – it being almost a metaphor for the increasingly cultured and affluent households in which it resided. Thus the 'Drawing Room Symphony' was born and became a staple ingredient of domestic music-making for well over a century. One can find numerous references to the typical family concert, several generations surrounding the piano, in mid-Victorian literary fiction. Even as late as the 1930s, the novelist

E. F. Benson made numerous references to duet playing in his celebrated *Mapp and Lucia* series.

However, the duet transcription should be viewed as far more than just a genre to satisfy the 'entertainment' needs of the well-off. Its significance lies in the fact that, through this medium, music that would otherwise remain generally unheard, became far more widely known and accessible. A piano duet transcription, in many ways, kept the music 'alive' in an age when a full orchestral performance was both a rare and exclusive event. Conversely, many orchestral works were first performed in their duet version, the success of which eventually lead to full performances at a later date. Sadly, some composers only ever heard some of their major orchestral work on the piano.

In the introduction it was stated that much of this genre of music has been either forgotten or lost. Of course, 'lost' is a term open to interpretation. Certainly, the vast majority of the transcriptions discussed in this book are no longer in print and generally unavailable to borrow, being systematically discarded from both public institutions and publisher stock rooms over the last fifty years or so. However, it would be wrong to suggest that this music is lost in the sense that it no longer exists. The music can be found in various national collections, large private collections and, more sporadically, in countless attics, cellars and dusty music cupboards. There is also a thriving antiquarian book market where many scores can be purchased. The problem lies in being able to locate particular pieces and gain suitable access to them.

The emergence of new technology at the end of the nineteenth century – that of sound recording – and its growth in the next century had a significant part to play in the demise of the piano as the focal point for domestic music making, especially the performing of duet transcriptions. Ironically, it is the emergence of a new twenty-first century technology that offers us a chance to rediscover the whole history of this genre.

In recent years, a growing number of internet sites have been established, offering digitized versions of old (public domain) music scores. One of the first companies to offer this service was Elibron (www.elibron.com), part of Adamant Media, an American company founded in 1999. Claiming to hold the world's largest collection of electronic books and music scores, produced in cooperation with the Russian State Library and the Russian National Library, over forty thousand scores were recently listed of all music types. The non-commercial International Music Score Library Project (http://imslp.org/wiki/Main_Page) is currently attempting to create a 'virtual library' containing all public domain musical scores. PDF files of scanned music can be freely downloaded. The IMSLP also encourages users of the site to comment upon and discuss the music to encourage greater awareness and analysis. At the time of writing, over twenty thousand scores were freely available, including a large variety of duet arrangements. A similar site is www.pianophilia.com. Various forums encourage discussion about the music and allow members to request particular pieces of music which then can be uploaded to the site by members and subsequently downloaded by others.

Of particular interest on this latter site is an area dedicated to transcriptions. The 'Opus Transcribisticum' database, maintained by Ludwig Madlener, is 'dedicated to all music lovers who enjoy this long disregarded, little valued and almost forgotten musical genre. Its purpose is to preserve the names of many musicians who were often highly regarded in their times as composers, instrumentalists, professors or simply as music teachers and who, with their adaptations or arrangements, introduced the works of the great masters to a wider public in times lacking the possibilities of electronic media.' The database is constantly being updated as new transcriptions come to light.

Although national institutions such as the British Library hold numerous out of print music scores – some hundreds of years old – in general they cannot be borrowed and can only be viewed in the institutions themselves. There is very limited access to some of the more precious scores. These restrictions make serious study, let alone performance, extremely difficult. However, there is now a concerted move to make more musical material available via the internet in the future. This follows on from the pioneering work of the Sibley Music Library at the Eastman School of Music, University of Rochester, USA (www.esm.rochester.edu/sibley). Holding well over three quarters of a million items, including a substantial collection of duet transcriptions, it is one of the largest specialist music libraries in the world. Not only has it scanned and made a vast amount of material available already, but has funding to further expand the service, even allowing for specific requests from musicians and scholars.

Discussing the value of such collections, Paul O. Kristeller states that:

'Ideas, styles and motifs of the past may lose their appeal in a certain period or climate of opinion, but this must not be final, for they may regain their validity at another time and under different conditions. It is therefore important to preserve in libraries and museums the monuments of past thought and productive activity. They should always be studied by specialists, for antiquarian purposes, if you wish, but they may also regain their life and relevance, as it were, at any time and what was dead or unknown to one generation may suddenly and unexpectedly become important for the next.'[91]

This argument holds particularly true for the piano transcription. Easy access to material – and one can imagine that in some future era, virtually everything that has ever been published will be freely available in digitised form – promotes further study and leads to an even greater level of understanding.

The recording industry itself – once so maligned by enthusiasts of the transcription – may also play a significant role in elevating the genre once again. Given that the vast majority of the classical repertoire has now been recorded several times over, in ever-increasingly spectacular sound, recording companies – especially smaller ones catering for a niche market – are looking for new and interesting works to record. Thus we now have a growing number of recordings which offer 'original versions', 'alternative versions' and transcriptions (in many different forms) of familiar pieces of music.

In her introductory notes to her recording of Mahler's Sixth and Seventh Symphonies arranged for piano duet, Evelinde Trenkner, tongue firmly in cheek, asks:

'Are such performances symptomatic of a new trend back to the four-handed arrangements we thought had been laid to their permanent rest in the musical graveyards of the nineteenth and early twentieth centuries? Or is it only that a few curio fetishists are carrying out their devotions in worthless experiments with the wrong materials?'[92]

What is undoubtedly clear is that a growing number of piano duet performers are recording an expanding repertoire of duet transcriptions to satisfy an increasing demand for them. It is not without significance that the vast majority of piano duet transcription recordings that are listed at the end of this book in the Selected Discography have been made during the last two or three years. This trend is almost certain to continue in the future as there is a whole catalogue of works waiting to be rediscovered and recorded.

As a genre, the 'Drawing Room Symphony' offers us the chance to explore the symphonic repertoire in a way which was very much normal practice in the previous two centuries. As we listen to a piano duet performance of a symphony by Bruckner or Tchaikovsky for example, we are, in a sense, transported aurally back in time. We are hearing the work as the composer probably first heard it as well as the first public audiences in many cases. New works were discussed and critically analysed often on the strength of these performances alone. In recent years there has been a marked swing towards 'authentic' performance – rarely will one hear a full orchestra play a Haydn symphony, for example, the forces employed being scaled back to suit a more scholarly approach. Similarly, listening to Beethoven piano sonatas on a fortepiano rather than the modern concert grand gives us a different perspective from which to appreciate the music. Perhaps the duet transcription should be seen in a similar light – part of the 'authentic' movement, with its own innate validity. Indeed, classical music thrives upon the fact that we desire to hear different and new interpretations of the major works of the repertoire.

We certainly know that a great many composers learnt the classical repertoire by means of the transcription – either by studying it or playing it for pleasure and there can be few who would argue against the merits of the transcription in this respect. Today, we have easy access to recorded performances and orchestral scores but, ultimately, studying music in this way is a passive activity. Performing a transcription (either for two or four hands) gives us the opportunity to actively engage with the music – which, many might argue, is far more preferable and beneficial to learning.

The production of transcriptions encouraged the collaboration of a number of composers – Bruckner and Mahler, Debussy and Stravinsky, Ravel and Delius to name but a few. Indeed, the piano was often the focal point as groups of composers met with each other, both formally and informally. We can only speculate upon the influences each composer had on the other but it is clearly evident that a 'cross-fertilisation' of ideas was taking place as composers performed transcriptions of their work with colleagues. Moreover, this collaborative music-making, in both a social and academic context, played a part in helping to forge and develop several national styles, the Russian and French schools, perhaps, being the most obvious.

Unbelievable as it may seem today, a number of J. S. Bach's original manuscripts were sold for scrap paper after his death. Indeed, the whole history of music is littered with similar stories which today seem either incredulous or inexplicable. Perhaps we should not therefore be surprised that the 'Drawing Room Symphony' saw such a demise in the twentieth century. Musical taste and fashion change constantly, as do the perceptions of musical value and importance. Those selling Bach's manuscripts for a little loose change saw nothing wrong in their actions. Indeed Bach's music was almost to disappear itself until its revival in the mid-nineteenth century. Similarly, those discarding volume upon volume of piano transcriptions in the mid-twentieth century, did so in the belief that they had had their time and had become an irrelevance.

Without doubt, the genre of the piano duet transcription is now in the process of re-evaluation and there is a resurgence of interest in the huge body of works available. It can stand proud, phoenix-like, alongside the rest of the piano repertoire. Yet there is still a huge task facing music scholars if we are to fully uncover the historical background to many of these arrangements and those who dedicated their lives to the art of the transcription. Hopefully, this book has made some contribution to this.

Selected Bibliography

Bozarth, George S: The Brahms-Keller Correspondence (University of Nebraska Press 1996)

Brown, A. Peter: The Symphonic Repertoire (Indiana University Press 2003)

Christensen, Thomas: Four-Hand Piano Transcription and Geographies of Nineteenth-Century Musical Reception (Journal of the American Musicological Society 1999 vol.52 no.2)

Cooke, Deryck: The Bruckner Problem Simplified (Musical Times Jan. 1969)

Davies, Stephen: Transcription, Authenticity and Performance (British Journal of Aesthetics Vol.28 No.3, Summer 1988)

Davies, Stephen: Versions of Musical Works and Literary Translations in Philosophers on Music: Experience, Meaning and Work ed. Kathleen Stock (Clarendon Press 2007)

Ferguson, Howard: Keyboard Duets from the 16th to the 20th Century for One and Two Pianos (Oxford University Press 1995)

Grange, Henry-Louis de la: Gustav Mahler (Oxford University Press 1999)

Harrandt, Andrea: Students and friends as 'prophets' and 'promoters': the reception of Bruckner's works in the *Wiener Akademische Wagner-Verein* in Perspectives on Anton Bruckner edited by Crawford Howie (Ashgate 2001)

Hildebrandt, Dieter: A Social History of the Piano (Hutchinson 1988)

Hinson, Maurice: The Pianist's Guide to Transcriptions, Arrangements and Paraphrases (Indiana University Press 1990)

Johnson, Stephen: Bruckner Remembered (Faber and Faber 1998)

Kentner, Louis: Piano (Kahn & Averill 1991)

Larner, Gerald: Maurice Ravel (Phaidon Press Ltd, 1996)

Lott, R. Allen: From Paris to Peoria – How European Piano Virtuosos Brought Classical Music to the American Heartland (Oxford University Press Inc. USA 2003)

McGraw, Cameron: Piano Duet Repertoire: Music Originally Written for One Piano Four Hands (Indiana University Press 1981)

Moshevich, Sofia: Dmitri Shostakovich, Pianist (McGill-Queens University Press 2004)

Northrop Moore, Jerrold: Edward Elgar – a Creative Life (Clarendon Paperbacks 1999)

Orenstein, Arbie: A Ravel Reader: Correspondence, Articles, Interviews (Columbia University Press 1990)

Poznansky, Alexander/Langston, Brett: The Tchaikovsky Handbook: Volume 2 (Indiana University Press 2002)

Roberge, Marc-André: From Orchestra to Piano: Major Composers as Authors of Piano Reductions of Other Composers' Works (Notes – New York Music Library Association Vol.49 No.3 1993)

Samson, Jim: Virtuosity and the Musical Work: The Transcendental Studies of Liszt (Cambridge University Press 2003)

Scherer, F. M: Quarter Notes and Bank Notes: The Economics of Music Composition in the Eighteenth and Nineteenth Centuries by (Princetown University Press 2004)

Scruton, Roger: The Aesthetics of Music (Oxford University Press 1997)

Smith, Barry: Frederick Delius and Peter Warlock: A Friendship Revealed (Oxford University Press 2000)

Small, Christopher: Music, Society and Education (Wesleyan University Press 1996)

Todd, R. Larry: Mendelssohn (Cambridge University Press 1993)

Walker, Alan: Reflections on Liszt (Cornell University Press 2005)

Walsh, Stephen: Stravinsky: A Creative Spring: Russia and France 1882-1934 (University of California Press 2002)

Wilde, David: Transcriptions for Piano from Franz Liszt – The Man and His Music (Barrie and Jenkins 1970)

Selected Discography of Four-Hand Piano Transcriptions

The Naxos series of Brahms' four-hand piano works and transcriptions is currently running to 17 volumes. As an example, Volume 7 includes the transcriptions of the Second and Third Symphonies. **Naxos 8.554822**

The Brahms Piano Concerto No. I in its four-hand guise. **Summit 184**

This CD is the only available recording of one of Bruckner's symphonies arranged for four hands. **Musikproduction Dabringhaus und Grimm MDG330059I-2**

Debussy's four-hand arrangements, including Tchaikovsky's *Swan Lake* and Wagner's *The Flying Dutchman* Overture. **Marco Polo 8.223378**

Debussy's own four-hand arrangements of *Nocturnes* and *La Mer.* **BIS CD-526**

Debussy's teenage *Symphonie* together with other duet arrangements. **Quartz QTZ2048**

Duet arrangements of the music of Delius made by Peter Warlock. **BIS CD-1347**

The *New World* Symphony by Dvořák and the *Scottish* Symphony by Mendelssohn – transcriptions by the composers. **The Divine Art 25028**

Gershwin's two piano version of *An American in Paris* coupled with Grainger's *Porgy and Bess Fantasy.* **EMI Encore 5752242**

The duet transcription of *The Planets* made under the supervision of the composer, Holst. **Black Box CDBBM1041**

Bruno Walter's transcription of Mahler's First Symphony. **Praga Records CPRAGSA197**

Chitose Okashiro's remarkable transcription of Mahler's First Symphony – included here as it can be directly compared to the Walter version. **Chateau CI0001**

Mahler's Sixth and Seventh Symphonies transcribed by Zemlinsky and Cassella. **Musikproduction Dabringhaus und Grimm MDG3300837-2.** An alternative recording of the Sixth Symphony is also available on **Pepperland PEP05029**

Wonderful performances of Gershwin and Ravel, including the piano duet version of *Bolero*. **Divine Art DDA25057**

This recording also includes Ravel's own transcription of *Bolero* for two pianos. **Chandos CHAN 8905**

Duet arrangements made by Rimsky-Korsakov himself and his wife, Nadezhda Purgold. The performers state that the transcriptions made by Purgold are more 'intelligently' produced than those of her husband! **Linn CKD 294**

Scriabin's *Divine Poem* and *Poem of Ecstasy* transcribed by Lev Konyus. **Naxos 8.555327**

Symphony No. 4 by Shostakovich transcribed for four hands by the composer. **Chandos CHAN10296**

Stravinsky's piano duet version of the ballet *The Rite of Spring.* **Naxos 8.553386**

As well as offering an alternative reading of *The Rite*, this recording also includes several additional transcriptions – a number recorded for the first time in this format. **Wergo 6683 2**

Tchaikovsky's own transcription of *Capriccio Italien* plus Rachmaninov's arrangement of *The Sleeping Beauty* and Debussy's version of *Swan Lake*. **Philips 442-778-2**

Tchaikovsky's Fourth Symphony transcribed by Taneyev and *Romeo and Juliet* transcribed by Nadezhda Purgold. **The Divine Art 25020**

Tchaikovsky's Fifth Symphony arranged by Taneyev. **BIS CD-627**

 Tchaikovsky's own transcription of his Sixth Symphony. **Kontrapunkt 32204**

Notes

[1] Piano by Louis Kentner (Kahn & Averill 1991) p.169

[2] www.musicweb.uk.net/classrev/2003/Jun03/Mahler1piano.htm

[3] quoted from Gresham College lecture 'Chamber Music Fights Back' given by Piers Hellawell 22/2/02

[4] A Social History of the Piano by Dieter Hildebrandt (Hutchinson 1988) p.11

[5] The Aesthetics of Music by Roger Scruton (Oxford University Press 1997) p.452

[6] Letter to Brahms January 1886 quoted in The Brahms-Keller Correspondence ed. George S. Bozarth (University of Nebraska Press 1996) p.90

[7] Vaughan Williams Essays edited by Byron Adams and Robin Wells (Ashgate Publishing Ltd. 2003) p. 3

[8] Four-Hand Piano Transcription and Geographies of Nineteenth-Century Musical Reception by Thomas Christensen (Journal of the American Musicological Society 1999 vol.52 no.2) p.262

[9] see Orchestral Technique: A Manuel for Students by Gordon Jacob (Oxford University Press 1931)

[10] see article by Michael Steinberg in The Beethoven Quartet Companion (University of California Press 1994) p.146

[11] Introduction to 'The Schubert Song Transcriptions for Solo Piano: The Complete Schwanengaesang (Liszt) by Andrew Walker (Dover Publications Inc. 1999)

[12] from article 'The Gregarious Art of Music' (Australian Musical Times April 1927)

[13] see Queer Episodes in Music and Modern Identity (University of Illinois Press 2002) p.170

[14] quoted in preface notes written by Peter Bartók for piano transcription of the 'Concerto for Orchestra' by Bartók (Boosey & Hawkes 2001)

[15] The Aesthetics of Music by Roger Scruton (Oxford University Press 1997) p.454

[16] Piano Duet Repertoire: Music Originally Written for One Piano Four Hands by Cameron McGraw (Indiana University Press 1981) p.x

[17] quoted from Gresham College lecture 'Chamber Music Fights Back' given by Piers Hellawell 22/2/02

[18] A Social History of the Piano by Dieter Hildebrandt (Hutchinson 1988) p.65

[19] see notes by Ates Orga for CD Johannes Brahms Four Hand Piano Music Vol. 1 (Naxos 8.553139)

[20] see essay by L. Michael Griffel in The Cambridge Companion to Schubert edited by Christopher H. Gibbs (Cambridge University Press 1997) p.194

[21] article in 'New York Times' December 1994

[22] quoted in 'Notes' (Music Library Association) December 1976 p.415

[23] quoted from Gresham College lecture 'Chamber Music Fights Back' given by Piers Hellawell 22/2/02

[24] see The Cambridge Companion to Haydn edited by Caryl Clark (Cambridge University Press 2005) p.14

[25] quoted in Sergei Rachmaninov by Sergei Bertensson and Jay Leyda (Indiana University Press 2001) p.35

[26] see notes by John Warrack for CD Tchaikovsky Fantasy (Philips 438 938-2)

[27] Gustav Mahler by Henry-Louis de la Grange (Oxford University Press 1999) p.23

[28] quoted in notes for 'Name the Tonality' (2005-2006) education programme, Cincinnati Symphony Orchestra

[29] Frederick Delius and Peter Warlock: A Friendship Revealed edited by Barry Smith (Oxford University Press 2000) p.120-121

[30] Quoted in an article by Michael Steinberg in The Beethoven Quartet Companion (University of California Press 1994) p.146

[31] see The Critical Reception of Beethoven's Compositions by His German Contemporaries by Wayne M. Jenner (University of Nebraska Press, 2001) p.33

[32] Richard Wagner's Prose Works transl. William Ashton Ellis (Routledge 1899) Vol 4 p.325

[33] Four-Hand Piano Transcription and Geographies of Nineteenth-Century Musical Reception by Thomas Christensen (Journal of the American Musicological Society 1999 vol.52 no.2) p.257

[34] Piano Duet Repertoire: Music Originally Written for One Piano, Four Hands by Cameron McGraw (Indiana University Press 1981) p.xiii

[35] Life of Moscheles by Charlotte Moscheles (Hurst and Blakett 1873) p.295 reproduced by Elibron Classics 2005

[36] letter in Bodleian Library, Oxford quoted in article by R. Larry Todd (see website for the Library of Congress, Moldenhauer Collection)

[37] autograph letter in English in the Library of Congress quoted in article by R. Larry Todd (ibid.)

[38] Franz Liszt, An Artist's Journey: Lettres d'un bachelier ès musique, 1835-1841 translated by Charles Suttoni (Chicago University Press 1989) p.45

[39] Transcriptions for Piano by David Wilde from Franz Liszt – The Man and His Music (Barrie and Jenkins 1970) p.168

[40] Posters in the John Johnson Collection of Ephemera (Bodleian Library, Oxford)

[41] Letters of Franz Liszt Vol. 1 collected and edited by La Mara (H. Grevel and Co. 1894) p.273

[42] see From Rome to the End: Letters of Franz Liszt Volume 2 by Mara La Mara and Constance Bache (Kessinger Publishing 2004) p.307

[43] Reflections on Liszt by Alan Walker (Cornell University Press 2005) p.11

[44] Virtuosity and the Musical Work: The Transcendental Studies of Liszt by Jim Samson (Cambridge University Press 2003) p.104

[45] From Orchestra to Piano: Major Composers as Authors of Piano Reductions of Other Composers' Works by Marc-André Roberge (Notes – New York Music Library Association Vol.49 No.3) p.927

[46] article dated 10 April 1840 and quoted in Four-Hand piano Transcription and Geographies of Nineteenth-Century Musical Reception by Thomas Christensen (Journal of the American Musicological Society 1999 vol.52 no.2) p.289

[47] Brahms by Malcom Macdonald (J. M. Dent 1990) p.60

[48] The Brahms-Keller Correspondence ed. George S. Bozarth (University of Nebraska Press 1996)

[49] ibid. p.xxxii

[50] Letters of Clara Schumann and Johannes Brahms edited by Berthold Litzman (Arnold 1927) vol.2 p.96

[51] The Brahms-Keller Correspondence ed. George S. Bozarth (University of Nebraska Press 1996) p.76

[52] ibid. p.80

[53] from notes for Brahms Fourth Symphony by Prof. W. Altmann (Ernst Eulenburg miniature score 1927)

[54] see introductory notes to Brahms Piano Concerto No. 1 (composer's original arrangement for piano four hands) by Ralph Neiweem and Claire Aebersold (Dover Publications Inc. 1996)

[55] ibid.

[56] The Music of Brahms by Michael Musgrave (Oxford University Press 1985) p.48

[57] see The Pianist's Guide to Transcriptions, Arrangements and Paraphrases by Maurice Hinson (Indiana University Press 1990) p.31

[58]The Brahms-Keller Correspondence ed. George S. Bozarth (University of Nebraska Press 1996) p.xxxiv

[59] Letter 308 to Vasili Bessell April 1873 – see The Tchaikovsky Handbook: Volume 2 ed. Alexander Poznansky and Brett Langston (Indiana University Press 2002). Herman Laroche (1845-1904) was a long-standing friend of Tchaikovsky who taught at both the Moscow Conservatory and St. Petersburg.

[60] Letter 289 to Modest Tchaikovsky – ibid.

[61] Letter 1366, 3 December 1879 – ibid.

[62] Letter to Taneyev 2 January 1878 – see The Life and Letters of Peter Ilich Tchaikovsky by Modest Tchaikovsky (Minerva Group Inc. 2004) p.255

[63] Tchaikovsky: Symphony No.6 by Timothy L. Jackson (Cambridge University Press 1999) p.17

[64] ibid.

[65] This is the only UE Bruckner duet arrangement which remains in print today. UE also published J. Schalk duet arrangements of the Second, Fifth and Seventh Symphonies.

[66] The Bruckner Problem Simplified by Deryck Cooke (Musical Times Jan. 1969) p.20-22

[67] quoted in Bruckner Remembered by Stephen Johnson (Faber and Faber 1998) p.125

[68] from notes by Michael Steinberg (San Francisco Symphony) www.sfsymphony.com

[69] quoted in Bruckner Remembered by Stephen Johnson (Faber and Faber 1998) p.154

[70] quoted in article 'Students and friends as 'prophets' and 'promoters'': the reception of Bruckner's works in the Wiener Akademische Wagner-Verein' by Andrea Harrandt in Perspectives on Anton Bruckner (Ashgate 2001)

[71] Gustav Mahler by B.Walter (Schoken Books 1957)

[72] Chateau Records C10001

[73] see notes by Gilbert Kaplan for CD Mahler Plays Mahler (Golden Legacy Recorded Music GLRS 101)

[74] Edward Elgar – a Creative Life by Jerrold Northrop Moore (Clarendon Paperbacks 1999) p.223

[75] From notes for CD Frederick Delius Arrangements for piano 4 hands by Peter Warlock (BIS CD-1347)

[76] quoted in A Ravel Reader: Correspondence, Articles, Interviews edited by Arbie Orenstein (Columbia University Press 1990) p.63

[77] The author was one of the pianists in this performance

[78] see notes by Evelinde Trenkner for CD Mahler Symphonies Nos. 6 & 7 arr. for Four Hands (MDG 330 0837-2)

[79] S. Prokofiev: Autobiography, Articles, Reminiscences by S. Shilifstein (University Press of the Pacific 2000) p. 23

[80] quoted in notes by Helena Bugallo for CD Stravinsky in Black and White (Wergo 6683 2)

[81] see notes by Peter Hill for CD Stravinsky – Music for Two Pianos (Naxos 8.553386)

[82] quoted in The Pianist's Guide to Transcriptions, Arrangements and Paraphrases by Maurice Hinson (Indiana University Press (1990) p.138

[83] quoted in notes by Helena Bugallo for CD Stravinsky in Black and White (Wergo 6683 2)

[84] see Stephen Walsh Stravinsky: A Creative Spring: Russia and France 1882-1934 (University of California Press 2002)

[85] From www.pianola.org – the website of the Pianola Institute

[86] Review of Fourth Symphony by Shostakovich (arr. for piano by the composer) Chandos CHAN 10296 in DHSC Journal No. 23 2005

[87] Dmitri Shostakovich, Pianist by Sofia Moshevich (McGill-Queens University Press 2004) p.145

[88] see The Pianist's Guide to Transcriptions, Arrangements and Paraphrases by Maurice Hinson (Indiana University Press 1990) p.109

[89] quoted in A Ravel Reader: Correspondence, Articles, Interviews edited by Arbie Orenstein (Columbia University Press 1990) p.490

[90] Maurice Ravel by Gerald Larner (Phaidon Press Ltd, 1996) p.203

[91] Renaissance Thought and the Arts by Paul Oskar Kristeller (Princeton University Press 1990) p.258

[92] see notes by Evelinde Trenkner for CD Mahler – Symphonies 6 and 7 (Musikproduktion Dabringhaus und Grimm MDG 330 0837-2)

The author gratefully acknowledges the scholarship of those cited in this book.

Ian Shepherd is a pianist and teacher of music, heading the Expressive Arts Faculty at a Norfolk school. Beginning piano studies at the age of seven, he developed a love of the piano duet repertoire as his studies progressed and has given many public performances of both solo and duet works. He studied at Sheffield University where he was awarded the Music Dissertation Prize and went on to post-graduate studies at Bretton Hall College. He holds Diplomas up to Fellowship level from The Associated Board of the Royal Schools of Music, Trinity College of Music and the London College of Music.

Cover illustration by the 'Punch' cartoonist John Leech (1817-1864) Back cover: Title page of Mahler's Second Symphony arranged for piano duet by Bruno Walter (1899)